The Book of Ornamental Knots

Books by John J. Hensel

Encyclopedia of Knots and Fancy Rope Work
    (with Raoul Graumont)
Square Knot Tatting Fringe and Needle Work
Splicing Wire and Fiber Rope
    (with Raoul Graumont)

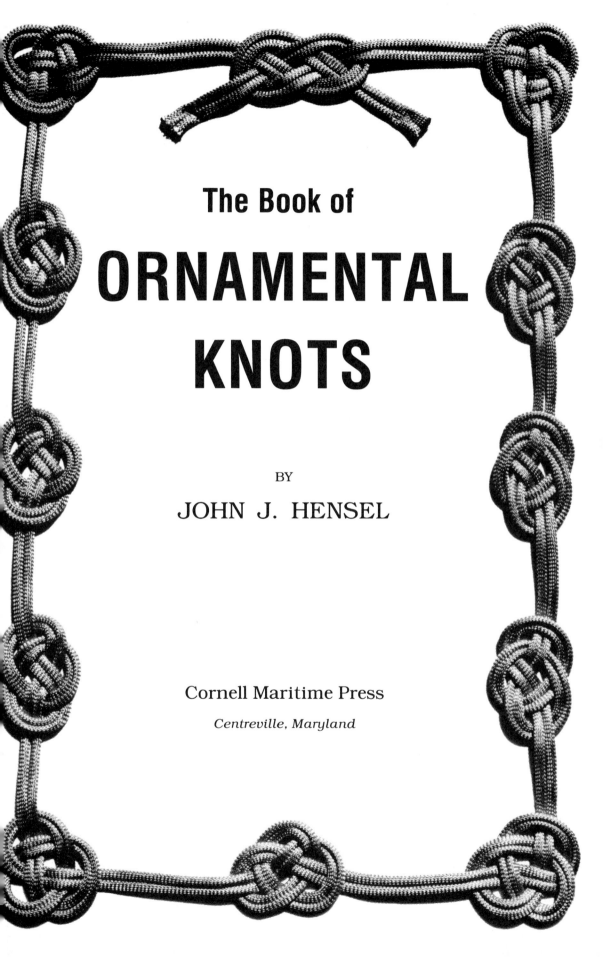

The Book of
ORNAMENTAL
KNOTS

BY

JOHN J. HENSEL

Cornell Maritime Press

Centreville, Maryland

An earlier edition of this work was published in 1973 by Charles Scribner's Sons.

Photography and design by John J. Hensel

Library of Congress Cataloging-in-Publication Data

Hensel, John.
    The book of ornamental knots / John Hensel. — 1st Cornell Maritime Press ed.
        p. cm.
    Reprint. Originally published: New York : Scribner, 1973.
    ISBN 0-87033-410-7
    1. Macramê. I. Title
[TT840.M33H46 1990]
746.42'22—dc20   89-77912
                                      CIP

Printed in the United States of America

First Cornell Maritime Press edition, 1990; second printing, 1994

Contents

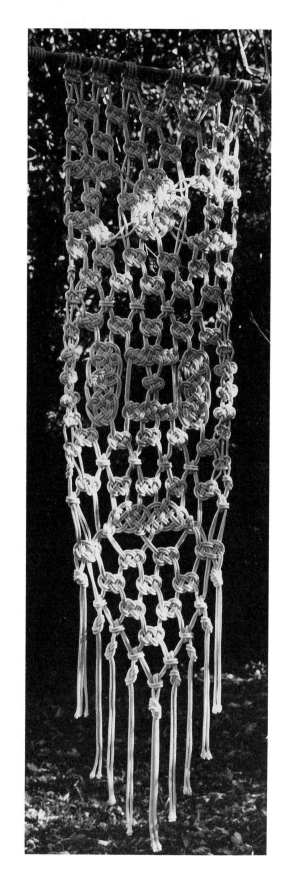

Room Divider

Preface

The use of rope or vines to serve the needs of man is as old as recorded history. Yet man's needs were not completely served by the ability to use cordage in assisting him to perform work. He began using it for amusement and for decorative purposes. Knotting as an art form reached its peak in the eighteenth and nineteenth centuries, principally executed by sailors in the sailing ship era. Their work required a degree of proficiency in the use of rope, and the material was usually available aboard ship. Therefore, it was inevitable that ornamental ropework became a rewarding method of whiling away the time on a long voyage. Many examples of their art are to be seen in museums today.

In recent years "square knotting" has become a popular form of this art. It is generally referred to as "macramé." This word (meaning the weaving and tying of lace) is presently used to describe any form of work which involves the tying, braiding, or weaving of cordage. One of the most fascinating types of knot tying is oriental ornamental ropework, around which this book is written. I found a great deal of interest in this branch of the art, especially because its basis is the ability to tie one basic and simple knot (although, in order to enhance the appearance of some designs illustrated here, a few accessory knots are included). This basic knot, the Carrick Bend (also called the Josephine Knot and Sailor's Breastplate Knot), is easy to learn and tie in many variations. It is decorative as well as functional. Articles in a simple form can be produced in a matter of minutes.

Before proceeding with the more complex designs which appear later in this text, a little time spent on the first few pages of fundamentals will be extremely useful in taking you on your journey into ornamental knots.

I wish to offer my fondest thanks to my wife, Dorothy, and my daughters, Thea, Karen, and Lillian, for their suggestions throughout the preparation of this book and their valuable help in editing and typing the manuscripts.

The Book of Ornamental Knots

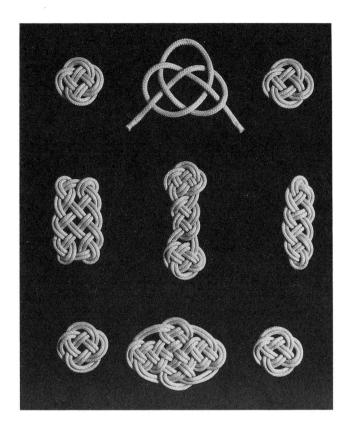

Introduction

The woven designs shown above all originate from the basic Carrick Bend (top center). All that is required to execute them is a little additional manipulation as described in picture form in this book.

The knot weaves may be mounted either singly or in groups, and in this manner make attractive wall hangings or tabletop displays. They may be mounted on a surface of white or colored material or directly on a wall. The cords or rope forming the designs may be white or a contrasting color to comple-ment the background, which will greatly enhance the appearance of the finished work.

The above designs were made with ¼-inch-diameter rope (clothesline size), and the examples range from 3 to 9 inches long by 2 to 5 inches in width. The basic Carrick Bend was made with ⅜-inch-diameter rope.

The picture on page 7 illustrates the arrangement of the working surface on which the knot designs are formed.

Explanation of the Weaving Process

Simply stated, the art of knot tying is basically a weaving operation. It is accomplished by manipulating the cordage by hand in a circular or curved fashion, as in Figure 1, rather than in straight lines as illustrated in Figure 2. In addition to this the cords are passed over and under each other, which is referred to as "locking" the weave. As in a piece of fabric, this over-and-under process is what holds the knots together.

The designs illustrated on the following pages are made by first laying out the cord or rope as shown in the Figure 1 on its respective page. Then you proceed to the second figure, observe the difference, and weave the rope into the position shown in the second figure. Follow this same procedure until all steps have been executed, thus completing the design or knot.

It should be noted that throughout this book the ends of the cord or rope which are being worked with in making the weaves have purposely been left much shorter than is the case in the actual work. The reason for this is that it is much simpler to follow a short end than a long one in the illustrations. The close-up photography used to show the details of the weaving did not permit inclusion of the added material.

1

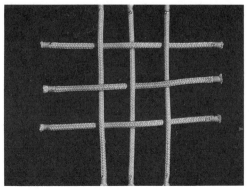

2

Correct Way to Double the Weave

The appearance of most knots is enhanced by the process of "doubling," illustrated in Figure 1. In many cases, the doubling rope can be woven into the design directly, as in Figure 1, page 33. The weaving of mats, as shown in Figure 12, page 114, is usually done with the single strand first and then the doubling process is performed. The adding of the additional rope strand is illustrated in Figure 3. At this point, it should be noted that when two or more strands are used weaving the design they must always be kept parallel to each other, as in Figures 1 and 3, and not crossed over as shown in Figures 2 and 4.

1

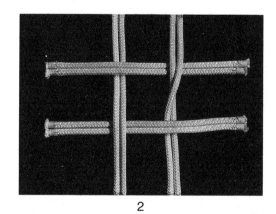

2

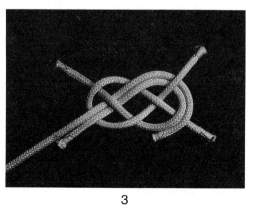

3

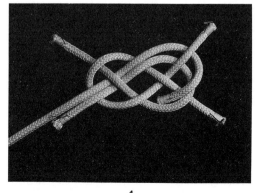

4

How to Start the Work

The articles illustrated in this book can be made from any type of rope or cordage generally available in a marine supply store, a hardware store, or a notions and trimmings store. A readily available material is clothesline. Most of the designs in this book were made with braided Dacron or nylon rope, ¼ inch in diameter. This material works very well in making the designs, follows the curves readily, stays in place when you shape the knot, and looks good when the article is completed. With this in mind it is preferable to use synthetic clothesline rather than cotton. The cotton material is rather stiff and you will find yourself fighting the cordage to make it form properly.

It is desirable to have an idea of the size of a finished article. Therefore, in all cases where this information applies, the length and width of the article will be given in inches. Most of the designs shown can be made with five to thirty feet of material.

To make the designs you should have a flat surface to work on, soft enough to hold pins to keep the work in place (see page 7). All the work in this book was made on a cloth-covered ceiling tile, which provides an excellent working surface and holds the pins firmly, yet enables the pins to be easily inserted and removed. Instructions for making such a board are given on page 24, and the method of mounting the ornamental knot is shown on page 26.

The rope is held in place with ordinary straight pins, or "T" pins as shown in Figure 1. The rope is pinned at a loop or intersection, or where necessary to hold the shape of the design, as shown in Figure 2.

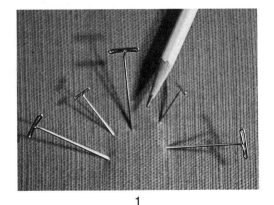

1

2

How to Handle the Rope

Some designs are made by pinning one end of the rope and working the design with the other end, as shown in Figure 1 and in more detail on page 72. Other designs are started by pinning the middle of the rope (or bight) and working with two ends, as shown in Figure 2 and in more detail on page 31.

In order to tie the knots properly, it is important to note from the picture whether the next move is to go over the next strand or under it. Therefore, the entire key to completing the designs is simply illustrated in Figures 2 and 3, and

will be the basic steps to follow throughout this book. Figure 2 shows the cord pinned at the top center. The cord on the left has been placed and pinned in its first working position. The cord on the right is then moved and pinned into the position shown in Figure 3. Once you become familiar with manipulating the cord or rope in this manner, you are ready to go to work. In Figure 4, the pencil points to the location where a knot weave should usually be pinned to hold the design in shape while the weaving process is being performed.

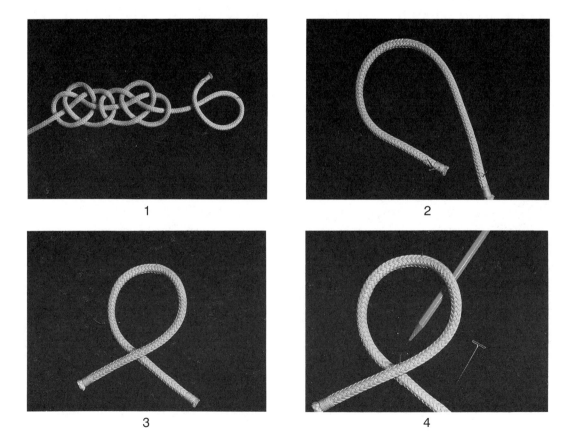

1

2

3

4

Doubling the Weave with a Single Strand

When a single strand is used to make the weave of a mat design, the basic knot is made first as in Figure 1. The basic pattern is then followed completely around, until the entire design has been filled with two strands. The beginning of this process is shown in Figure 2, the complete detail beginning on page 68.

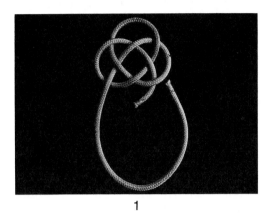

1

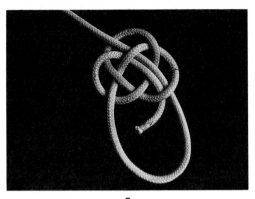

2

The Unlocked Weave

Some of the designs in this book require a portion of the weave to be in a temporarily unlocked position prior to completion of the knot. Carefully examine Figure 3 and compare it to Figure 4. Notice that the Carrick Bend in Figure 3 is in a locked position, whereas the Carrick Bend shown in Figure 4 is in the unlocked position. It is important to note that when working a knot design which has a move illustrated such as that in Figure 4, it is *very* important to pin it firmly in place, otherwise the pattern may be lost and you will have to start over again. Another illustration of this is shown beginning on page 64, Figures 1 through 9.

3

4

Pulling Up and Blocking the Knot Design

Perhaps the most important part of ropework, other than making the weave itself correctly, is the final operation, which is called "pulling up and blocking." In order to make a knot it is always necessary to have more material to work with than is actually required to produce the design in its final form. It is the removal of this surplus rope that is called "pulling up."

After the knot has been woven it is usually out of shape, having a loop in one place which is too large, and one too small elsewhere. The design must now be shaped or "blocked." Some of the blocking is done before the pulling up operation is started and the remainder is done while pulling up the knot.

At this point it should be noted that the pulling up and blocking procedure must be repeated two or three times in some cases, depending on the complexity of the design, before the knot is worked into its final symmetrical and smooth-flowing shape.

The novice who is beginning the work should practice the pulling up and blocking procedure on one of the simpler knots as illustrated in Figures 1 through 4 below.

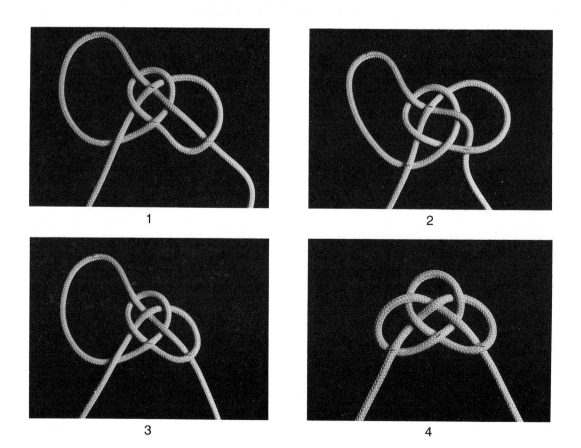

1

2

3

4

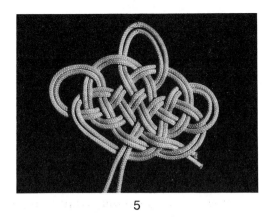

5

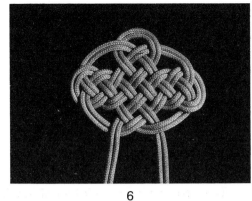

6

When the weaving of the knot has been completed it will frequently appear as shown in Figure 5. After the design has been shaped it will appear as shown in Figure 6. The steps between these two points are accomplished as follows.

First, remove *all* the pins used to hold the weave while forming it. Now begin to pull the surplus rope to the edges of the knot as shown in Figure 7, at the same time adjusting and shaping the design as shown in Figures 8 and 9.

When the knot has been manipulated so it appears reasonably symmetrical and most of the surplus has been worked to the edges, start the pulling up operation by beginning with the loose loop of the rope shown at the left-hand side (Figure 9), and retracing the woven pattern, removing the slack as you pull the doubled rope through the design as shown in Figure 10.

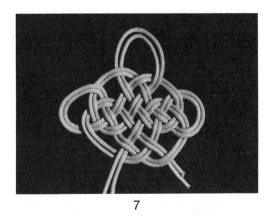

7

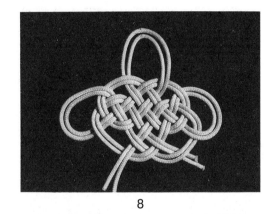

8

9

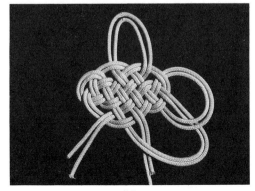

10

Proceed to remove additional slack (Figures 11-17). The knot pulled up and blocked is shown in Figure 18. It may be necessary to repeat this procedure again until the knot has been manipulated into a perfect and symmetrical shape. The best way to control and hold the design while performing the pulling up operation is to place the palm of one hand on the knot while pulling up the slack with the other (Figure 19).

Perhaps the most important thing to learn in knot tying is to develop the ability to see, in your mind's eye, only certain portions of the knot as it is being woven or pulled up. This is illustrated in Figure 20. Though the entire design is before you, the shaded portions are blanked out in your mind, and you are aware only of the remainder. This helps to avoid the confusion of having the weave look like a "bird's nest."

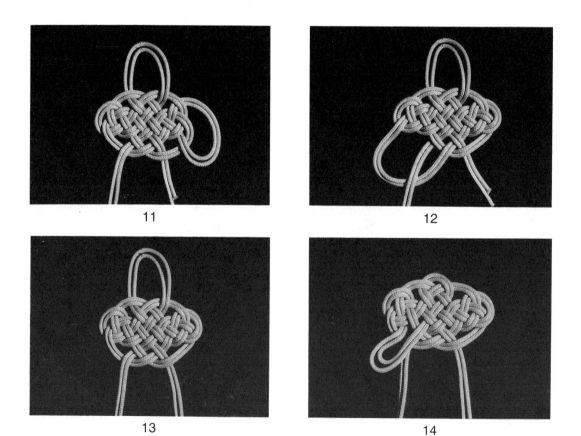

11

12

13

14

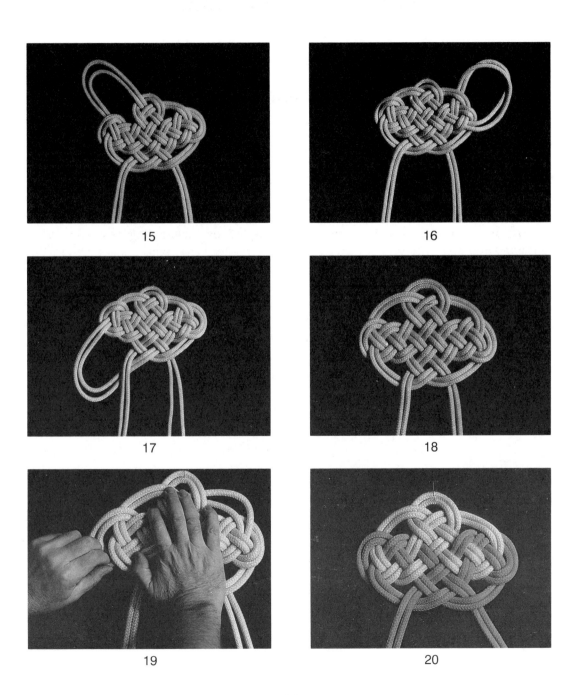

15

16

17

18

19

20

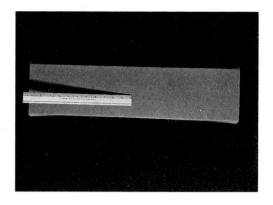

How to Make a Working Surface and Display Board

Many of the knot designs illustrated in this book should, for maximum effect, be displayed on an appropriate background color and be fastened to a surface to hold the design in shape. This is done by first cutting a piece of ceiling tile to the desired size. The one shown here is 6 inches wide and 24 inches high (Figure 1). Lay this on a piece of muslin or old sheet, fold the ends over, and staple or tack as shown in Figures 2 through 5. Now select the material you wish to use for the knot background. This can be either new or old, and may

be burlap, cotton, silk, nylon, or just about anything that strikes your fancy. A piece of sufficient size is cut and the muslin-covered piece laid on top of it (Figure 6). The edges are folded over and stapled or tacked (Figures 7-9). When completed, the back appears as in Figure 10. When turned over, the face appears as above, and is ready to have the knot design mounted (see page 26). The ceiling tile is an excellent material for holding and removing the pins while weaving knot designs (see illustration on page 7).

1

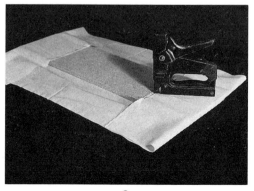

2

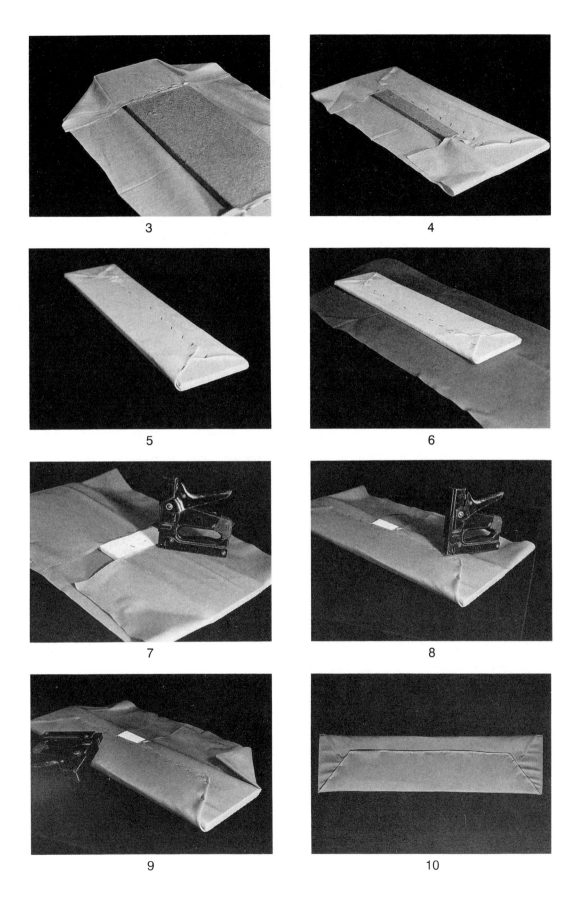

3

4

5

6

7

8

9

10

How to Mount the Knot on a Display Board

The backing material for a display board can be made of a ceiling tile, or, for a more rigid backing, a piece of plywood, either varnished, stained, or covered with material as shown on page 24. Another very effective background can be made by using a piece of driftwood. The arrangement of the knots can be varied, and some methods of display are shown on page 27.

Once the knot design has been made and the proper display board prepared, the last operation is to fasten the knot to the display board. This can be done either with a staple gun or with small nails and a hammer. If the ceiling tile material is used, the knot can simply be pinned to the surface. It will not be as firmly fastened as if a piece of wood were used. First make sure that the knot has been perfectly shaped by pulling up and blocking (see page 20). Now place it on the mounting board either in the exact center, or on one side, as desired (Figure 1). The knot should now be fastened by raising the top strands and fastening the bottom ones (Figure 2). The top strands are pushed back down on top of the bottom strands, which then conceal the fastening (Figure 3). The completed operation appears in Figure 4.

1

2

3

4

Suggested Mounting Layouts

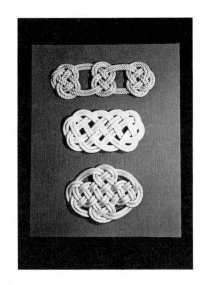

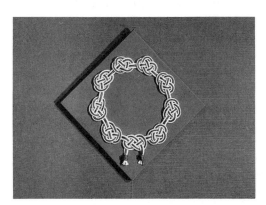

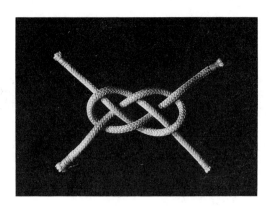

The Carrick Bend

This knot, also called the Josephine Knot and sometimes referred to as the Sailor's Breastplate Knot (because the air-hose lines on the front of a diving suit are so tied when not being used), is the principal and basic knot that will be used throughout this book. Once the tying of it is thoroughly learned, you will be able to make almost every knot design illustrated hereafter.

To practice making this knot, use two pieces of rope, each about 2 feet in length, either clothesline size or a little larger. Take one piece and pin it to the working surface (Figure 1). Next introduce the second piece to the design (Figure 2). Continue weaving and pulling the second piece through the first piece (Figure 3). Then continue as shown in Figure 4 and so on until the design has been completed as shown in Figure 8.

Some Carrick Bend designs are started by weaving the knot opposite to that shown. For example, in Figure 1 the rope pointing to the upper left should go under, rather than over, the other rope. This reversal of the design can be done by simply holding the book up to a mirror. Then proceed to follow the design. The entire knot will be tied in reverse.

The above design is 3 inches high and 8 inches long. The material required is two pieces of ½-inch-diameter rope, each 18 inches long.

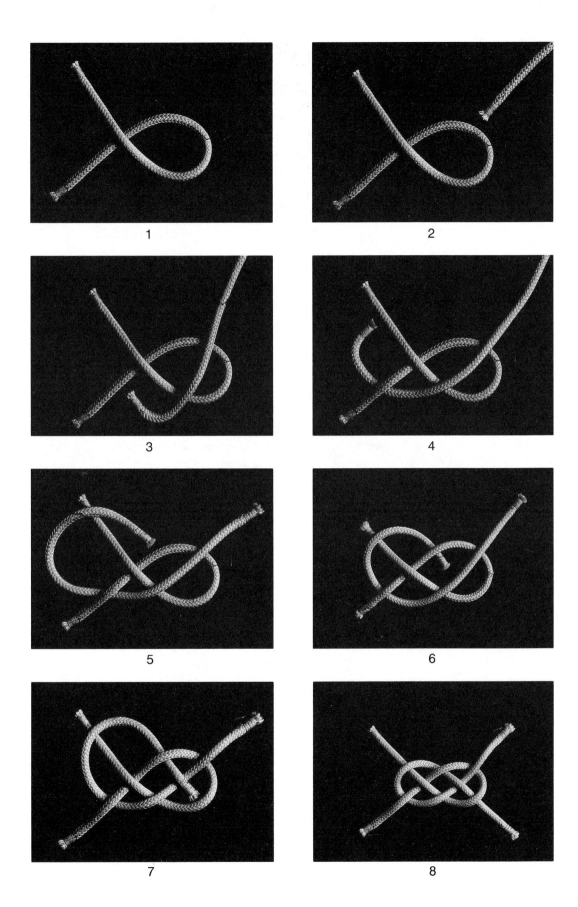

The Carrick Bend on a Bight

The bight of a rope is the middle point when it has been doubled over. This center point or middle of the loop is pinned to the working surface; the rope end on the left and the one on the right are now the working ends used for weaving the knot design.

The weave is made by first pinning the right-hand rope in the position shown in Figure 1. The left-hand end is now woven through the right-hand side (Figures 2-8).

The above design is 6 inches wide and 7 inches high. The material required is one piece of ½-inch-diameter rope, 3 feet long.

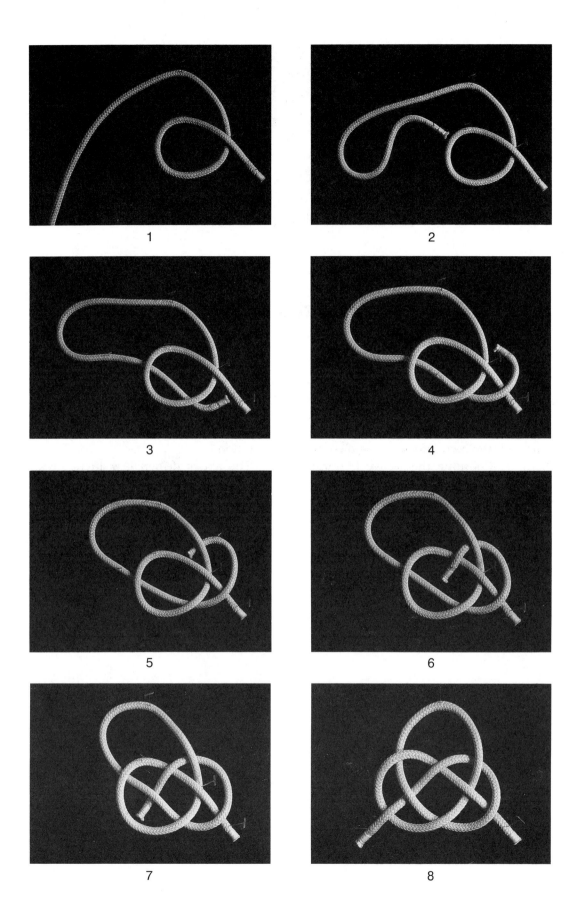

The Doubled Carrick Bend on a Bight

This design is made in the same manner as the single Carrick Bend on a Bight (page 30), except that the one shown here is made with the doubled ropes at one time. To start the weave, pin the center of the two ropes as shown in Figure 1. Continue the weave (Figures 2-7). The completed design pulled up and blocked is shown in Figure 8.

Note in Figure 4 that the piece of rope which follows the outside of the knot design has a longer distance to travel and therefore grows shorter as the knot design progresses. Because of this, the outside piece should be about one-fourth longer than the inside piece.

Note: See page 38 for additional explanation.

The above design is 7 inches wide and 10 inches high. The material required is one piece of rope 3½ feet long and one piece 4½ feet long, ½ inch in diameter. The longer rope will be the outside piece in weaving the pattern.

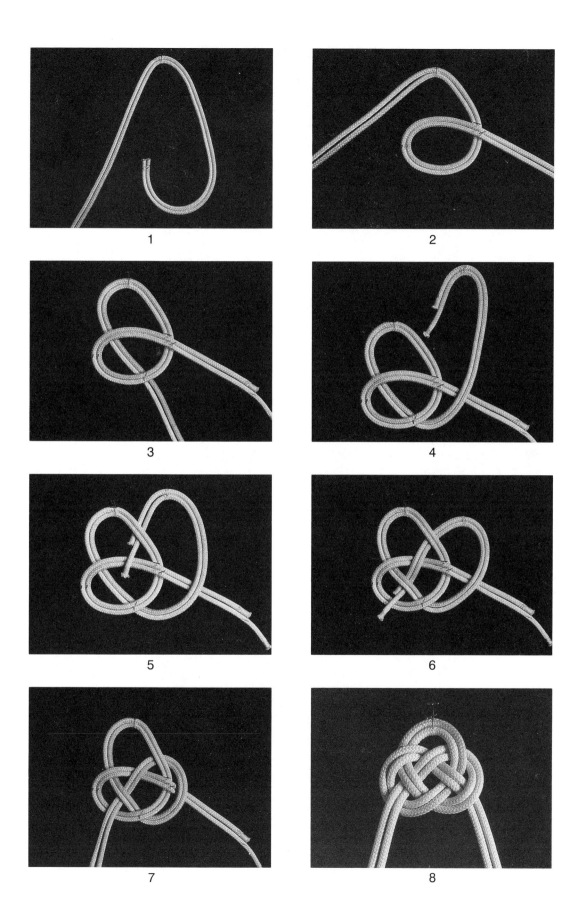

1

2

3

4

5

6

7

8

The Unlocked Carrick Bend and the Unlocked Carrick Bend on a Bight

This form of the Carrick Bend is used as the basic pattern to start many of the knot designs illustrated in this book. It should be carefully studied and compared to the standard Carrick Bend. Note in Figure 8 that the two bottom strands of rope, which would put the knot in a locked or self-supporting position, have been woven through the loops and must therefore be carefully pinned in order that the knot hold its shape and not lose the weave before the remainder of the design is completed.

This knot is made as shown in Figures 1 through 8. When you want to use two ropes to form the design, see page 64.

When the design to be made requires this knot to be started from a bight, then the knot is formed by starting from the middle of the rope as shown below; the knot is completed by starting from Figure 2 and continuing through Figure 8. An example of the knot being used in this manner is given on page 65.

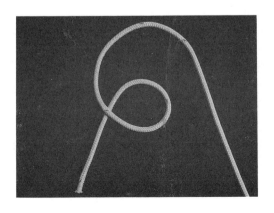

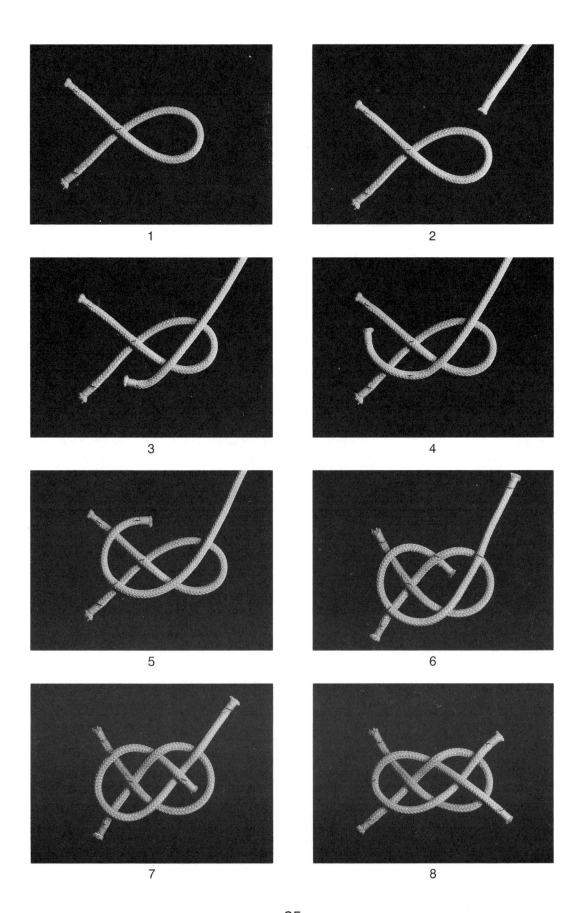

Doubling the Carrick Bend

The appearance of most knots is enhanced by adding another piece of rope to the design. The term used for this procedure is "doubling." The doubling operation can be done by using either the same color rope or a different color to suit the design or background as desired. For example, red rope can be used to construct the basic Carrick Bend. It can be doubled by using a white rope to complete the design. This can then be mounted on a board or other support in a contrasting color such as blue or black. Driftwood also makes an attractive background.

To weave the design shown above, first make the single Carrick Bend shown on page 28. This is left pinned to the working surface and the first piece of rope used in the doubling process is introduced to the design (Figure 1). Continue weaving (Figures 2-3). The first half has been completed in Figure 4. The second rope is introduced to the knot in Figure 5 and the weaving process is continued (Figures 6-8), with the completed design shown above. Made with four pieces of rope, each 15 inches long by 1/4 inch in diameter, the knot measures 7 inches wide by 4 inches high.

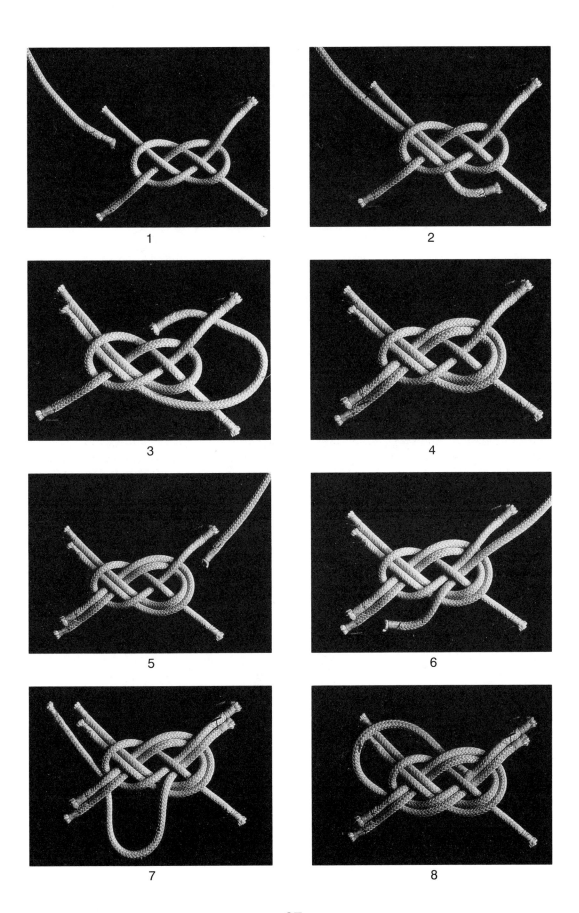

The Two-Strand Carrick Bend Weave

The doubled Carrick Bend and many of its variations can be made by weaving the knot with two strands at once, thereby completing the design in one basic weaving operation. This is much quicker than first weaving the basic knot with a single strand and then doubling it.

Note: The rope that is used on the outside of the knot should be longer than the one used on the inside, because the outside radius is greater than the inside radius and therefore requires more rope. If additional rope is not provided at the beginning, you will find that when the weave is partly finished you will have used up all the rope in half of each group. Turn to page 75, Figure 7, which illustrates this point. It is difficult to estimate how much rope to add because this depends on the thickness of the cord and the number of knots in the design. A rule of thumb for average conditions will be to increase the length of the outside rope by about one-fourth, or a little less.

The above design is 4 inches high and 9 inches long. The material required is four pieces of 1/2-inch rope, each 2 feet long.

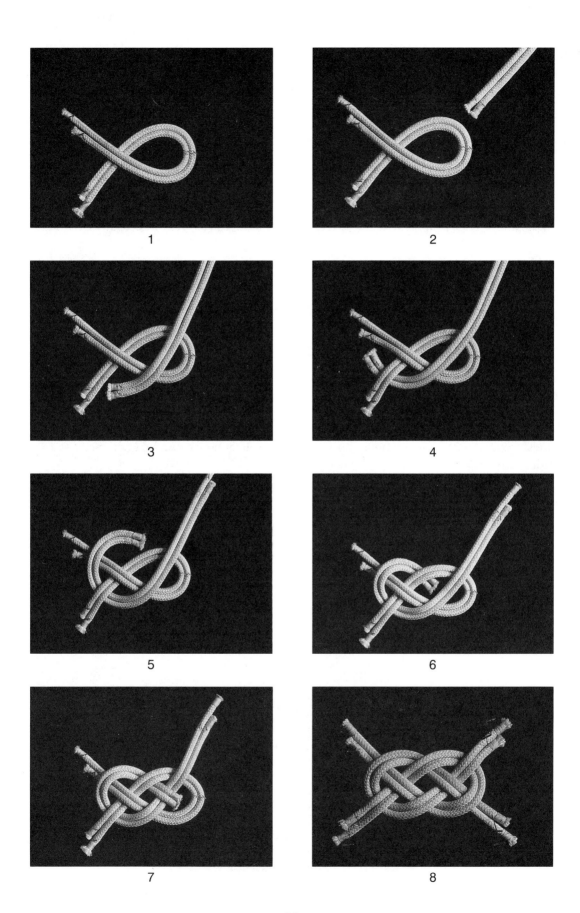

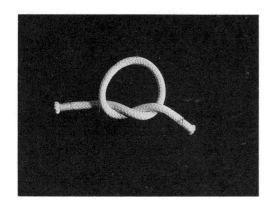 

The Overhand Knot

A few knots other than the Carrick Bend will be illustrated in this text, as they will be used in conjunction with the execution of Carrick Bend designs.

The Overhand Knot is shown in single and double form above and in triple form below.

The basic knot is tied as illustrated in Figures 1 through 4. Figures 5 through 8 show how to double the knot. It can also be tied by using either two or three pieces of rope at once. For an example of how it can be used, see page 42.

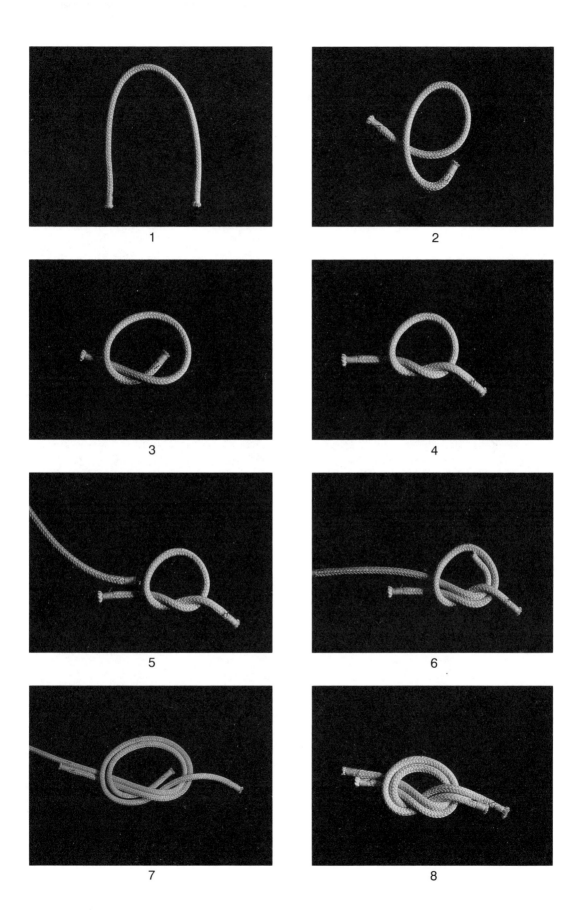

Interlocking Overhand Knots

This knot is formed by joining the bights of two Overhand Knots. To start, tie an Overhand Knot as shown on page 41 and pin it to the working surface as shown in Figure 1. The second rope is introduced to the design as shown in this same figure and another Overhand Knot is tied with this rope (Figure 6) before being pulled up tight. The knot pulled up is shown in Figure 7.

The doubled version of the knot (shown above right) measures 2½ inches wide and 7 inches high. The material required is four pieces of rope, each piece 16 inches long and ½ inch in diameter.

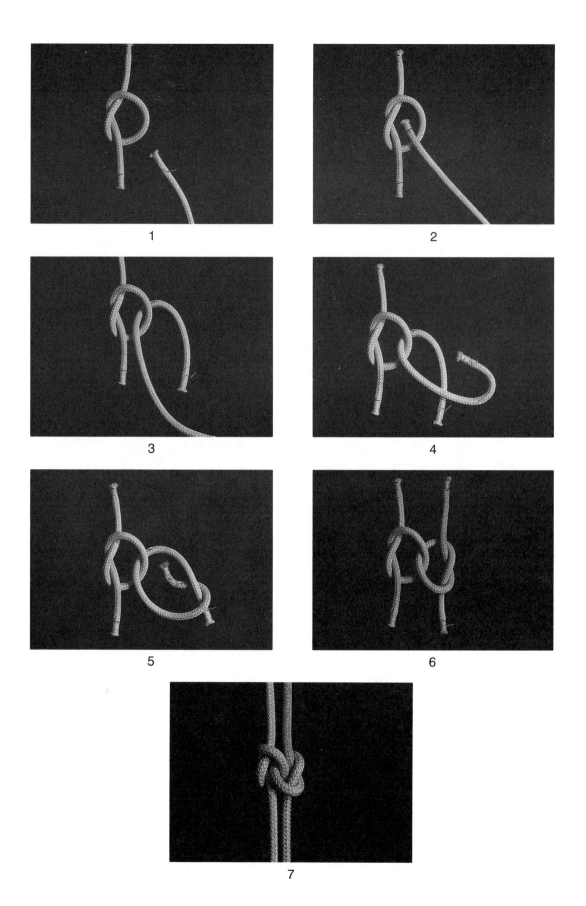

1

2

3

4

5

6

7

43

The Square Knot

This knot is familiar to most people and almost everyone knows how to tie it. This is perhaps one of the most frequently used knots in everyday life. It is used mainly to join two ends of rope, or in tying the ends of string on a package. It was also a familiar design used on ancient heraldic devices.

Frequently, when one attempts to tie the Square Knot the result, instead, is the Granny Knot, illustrated below. This error occurs when the two top rope ends are tied in a manner opposite to that illustrated in Figures 5 and 6.

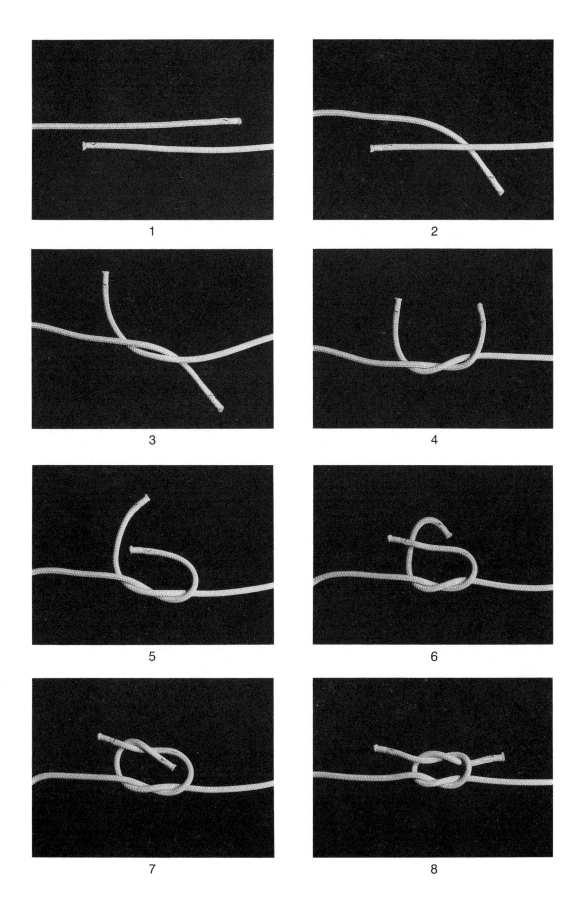

The Doubled Square Knot

This knot is made by first tying the single Square Knot illustrated on page 45, then pinning it to the working surface. The first doubling rope is introduced to the design as shown in Figure 2 and continues on to double half the knot (Figures 3-5). The second doubling rope is added as shown in Figure 5 and the weaving is continued (Figures 6-7). The completed knot is illustrated in Figure 7, but the design takes on a different appearance when the ends are brought together (Figure 8).

The above design is 5 inches high and 10 inches long. The material required is four pieces of ½-inch-diameter rope, each 18 inches long.

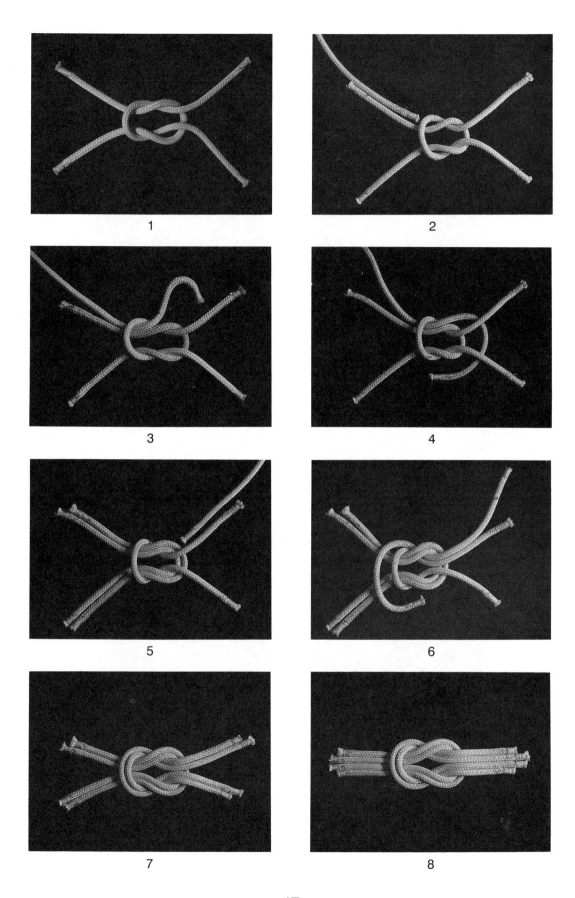

The Figure-of-Eight Knot

This knot is frequently used in ornamental work because it is simple to tie and has perfect symmetry. It can be made with either a single strand or with two as illustrated above. The doubled design, made with ½-inch-diameter rope, measures 2 inches wide and 7 inches high. The method of forming the single knot is illustrated in Figures 1 and 2.

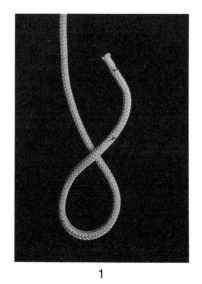

1

2

The Four-Strand Sennit Weave

This knot is generally used as part of other woven knot designs, such as Figure 4 on page 139 and the figures on page 171. The design above left measures 9 inches wide and 2 inches high.

The material required is two pieces of ¼-inch-diameter rope, each 3 feet long. Start the weave design by pinning one piece as shown in Figure 1, then begin the weave with the second piece as shown in Figures 2 through 4. The loop on the right is closed by repeating the steps shown in Figures 3 and 4, and will appear as above.

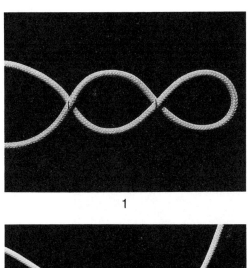

1

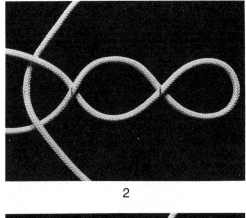

2

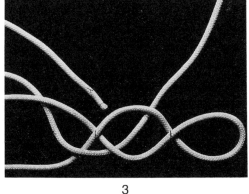

3

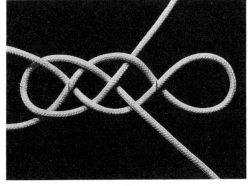

4

The Caterpillar Knot or Three-Strand Sennit Weave

This knot is also used as a terminal knot on wall hangings, as is the Figure-of-Eight Knot. It can be used when an elongated version of the Figure-of-Eight is desired. The design can be made any desired length by making additional crosses in the rope (Figure 3) and then continuing to repeat the weave (Figures 4-7). The completed basic weave is shown in Figure 8.

The doubled knot above right measures 11 inches wide and 2½ inches high. It was made with ½-inch-diameter rope, two pieces each 30 inches long.

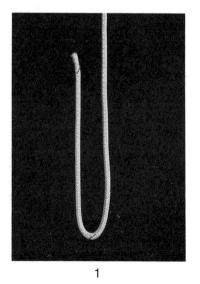

1

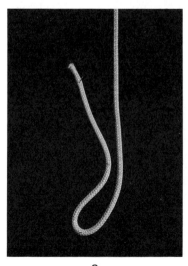

2

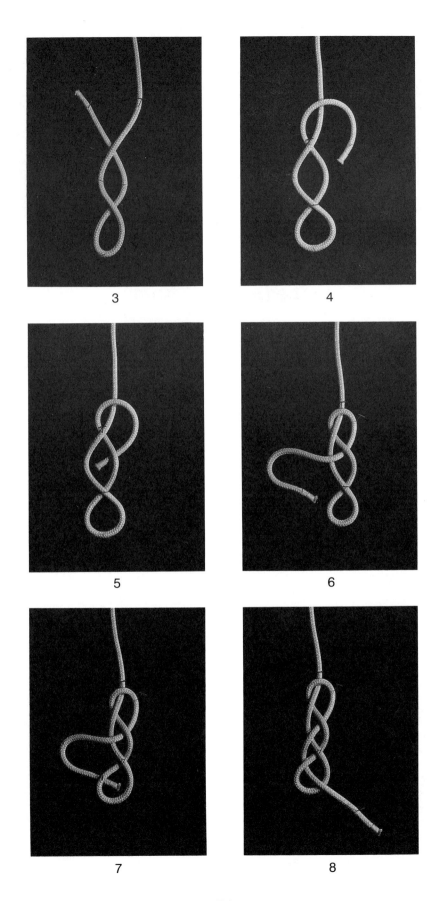

3

4

5

6

7

8

The Dragonfly Knot

This is an excellent example of oriental knotting and lends itself as an accent to Carrick Bend weaving. It appears difficult at first; however, in reality, it is one of the simpler knots to master. Once the weave has been learned it can be tied held in the hands without using a board and pins.

The doubled example, above right, measures 6 inches high and 3½ inches wide. It requires two pieces of ¼-inch-diameter rope, each 3 feet long.

The weave is started by pinning the rope in the center of the right-hand loop (Figure 1), and manipulating the bottom rope end (Figure 2). The upper end is now taken and the weave continued (Figures 3-9). At this point, slowly pull up the knot and work out the slack, holding its shape until it begins to look like Figure 10. The balance of the slack can now be worked out of the knot and additional slack can also be pulled into the top loop.

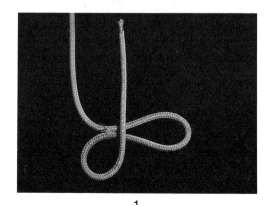

1

2

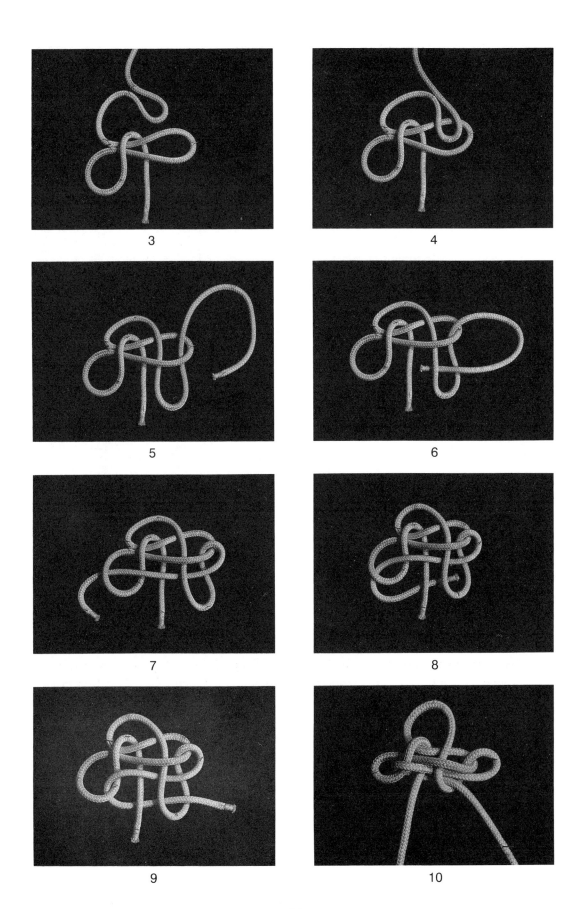

3

4

5

6

7

8

9

10

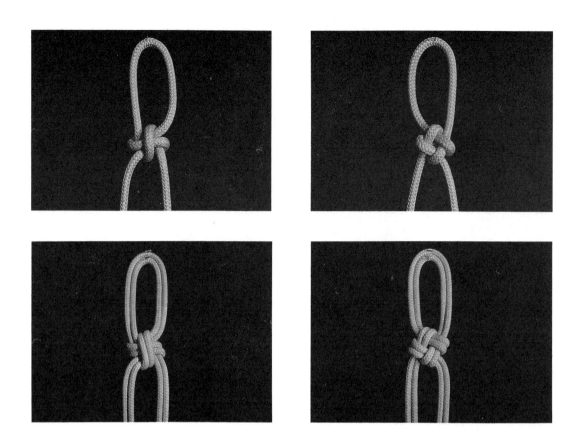

The Japanese Crown Knot

This is a nice-looking, compact knot. It is similar to the Dragonfly Knot but does not have the "ears" on each side. When viewed from the front, above right, the weave forms a rectangle. When turned around, above left, the back forms a cross. The top two pictures show the single weave; the bottom pictures above show the double weave.

The single knot, above right, measures 6 inches high and 2 inches wide. It was made with 1/4-inch-diameter rope, about 2 feet long.

To start, pin the right-hand end of the rope as shown in Figure 1. The remainder of the design is woven with the left-hand end of the rope (Figures 2-7). When pulled up, the finished knot will appear as in Figure 8, which is the back of the design. When turned over, it will appear as one of the pictures above right, depending on whether it was made with one or two ropes.

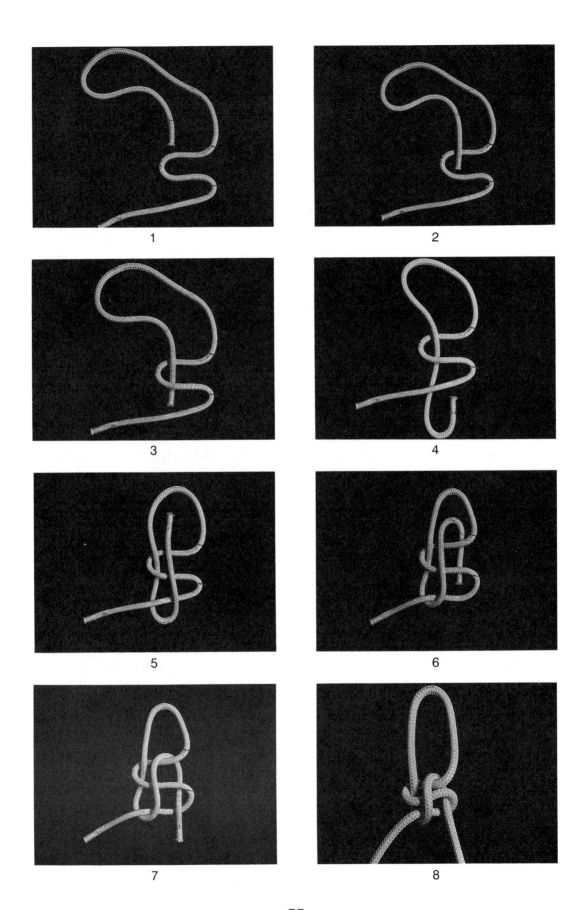

The Carrick Bend Turk's Head

This is perhaps one of the most widely known knot designs. Although tied in a different manner from the true Turk's Head, it so closely resembles it that only those expert in knot tying can tell the difference. This weave is very popular as the sliding knot used on Boy Scout neckerchiefs. It makes an attractive napkin ring or a bracelet, and can be used to decorate any cylinder, such as a lamp base, boat tiller, or flagpole.

The first step in forming the knot is to make the Carrick Bend coaster, as illustrated on pages 68 through 70, stopping when Figure 16 is reached. The knot will then appear as shown on page 57, Figure 1. At this point, remove the pins and pick the knot up in the left hand, as shown in Figure 2, putting your fingers through the center. With your right hand, work the rope into a round flat shape against your fingers (Figures 3-4). Pass one end of the rope throughout the knot (Figure 5). This will double the last single strand seen in the center of the weave. Basically the knot is now completed as a two-pass Turk's Head (Figure 6). The ends are sewn and cut off as illustrated on page 71, Figure 19.

The Turk's Head usually looks better when made with three passes rather than two. The knot can be tripled, adding another pass, by following the weave starting at Figure 5.

The triple design can also be made more easily by adding the third pass at the Figure 1 stage, prior to starting the operation shown in Figure 2.

If the knot is to be used on top of another object (Figures 7-8), then simply slip the Turk's Head over the object and tighten it up. When all the slack has been removed and the knot is very tight, the ends are cut off close to the edge of the weave to finish it. It is not necessary to sew the ends, because the knot when drawn up tight holds them in place.

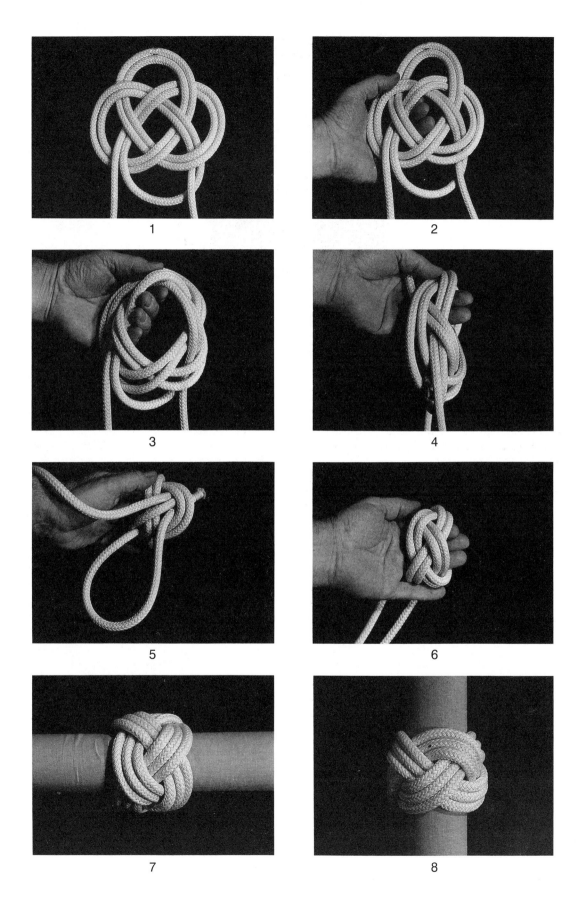

1

2

3

4

5

6

7

8

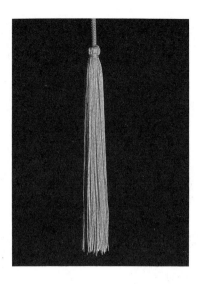

How to Make the Tassel

One method of finishing off a belt or wall hanging which lends a professional touch to the art of knotting is the tassel. The one illustrated above, which measures 10 inches, is about the right length for most purposes. However, it can be made longer or shorter as desired.

The material used is called "chainette," a term derived from the chain knot used in forming the braid of which it is made. It is most frequently seen on the cap of a school graduate. The material is usually sold on spools such as that shown in Figure 1.

To start the tassel, take this book and wind the chainette around it 60 times (Figure 2). Cut the chainette from the spool and place a temporary tie around the entire group of cords (Figure 3). Next, cut through all the cords with a scissors (Figure 4), which will yield a hank (Figure 5). This is then placed next to the rope ending on which the tassel is to be fastened (Figure 6). The rope end and hank of chainette are now joined

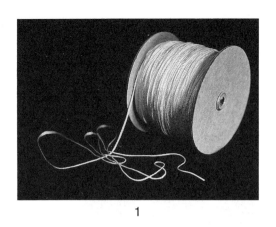

1

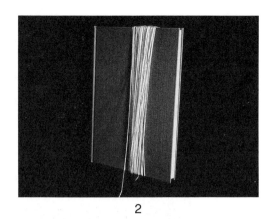

2

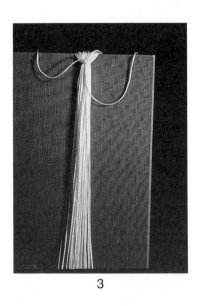

3

4

5

6

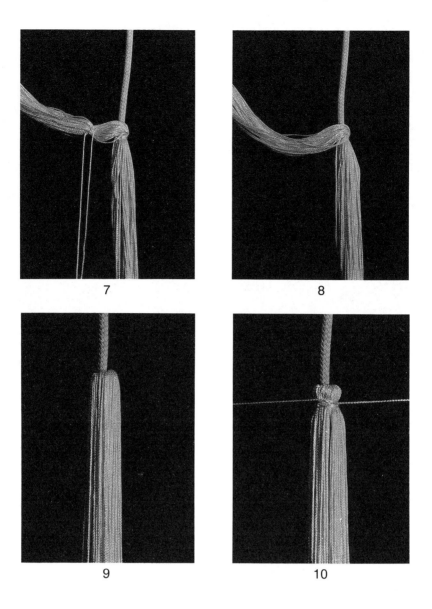

7

8

9

10

together (Figure 7). Spacing the chainette evenly around the rope end, place a permanent and tightly bound seizing around both rope ends and chainette, about one inch below the temporary tie. This wrapping (or seizing, as it is called) is shown in greatly enlarged detail on page 61.

At this point the temporary tie is cut (Figure 8) and the upper portion of the chainette hank is folded down around the lower portion (Figure 9). The chainette is now evened out around the rope end and another permanent seizing is placed around the tassel (Figure 10).

The chainette material comes in a great variety of colors and many rope and tassel color combinations can therefore be worked out.

To finish off the tassel, take a scissors and trim the bottom end of the chainette material until it is approximately even and straight.

How to Make a Seizing

It is frequently necessary to tie a group of cords together, or "seize" them, such as when forming a tassel. The seizing is generally formed with a small cord or string.

Wrap (three to six turns) the string around the material to be seized (Figure 1) and then form a Square Knot (see page 45) with the two ends (Figures 2-4).

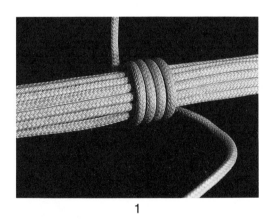

1

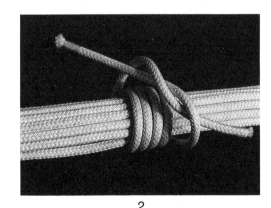

2

3

4

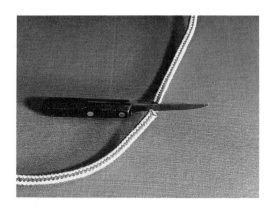

How to Make a Whipping

It is generally necessary when working with rope or cordage to secure the ends to prevent unraveling. This can be accomplished in several ways. When a design is being fashioned, it is only necessary to have the ends temporarily secured, which can be done by using a small piece of transparent adhesive tape. Another temporary method which is only done on the man-made fibers is to cut the rope and then heat the ends with a match, which will melt the fibers together and form a solid end, or the rope can be cut with a red-hot knife as shown above right.

When a permanent finish is desired, a whipping should be applied, such as the one illustrated above left. It is made with thin twine. The end is wrapped tightly to a length which equals the diameter of the rope.

It is made by placing the twine as shown in Figure 1, proceeding to make the desired number of wraps, and then putting the end through the loop as in Figure 8. The other end on the left-hand side is now pulled until the right-hand loop and twine end are pulled under the wrappings. The two ends are now cut off short to finish.

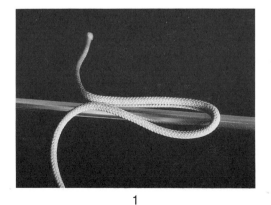

1

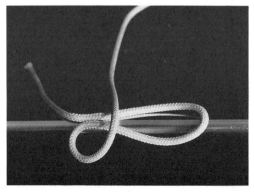

2

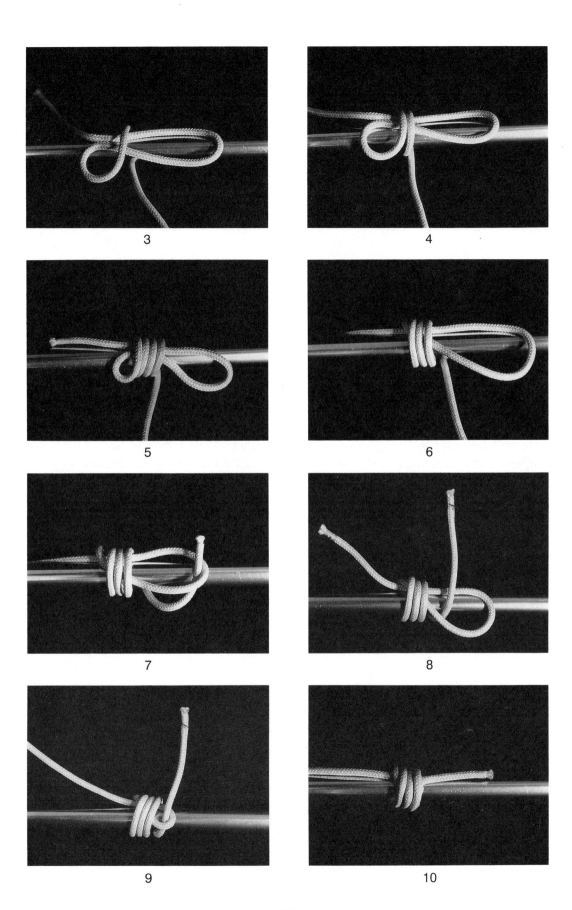

3

4

5

6

7

8

9

10

63

 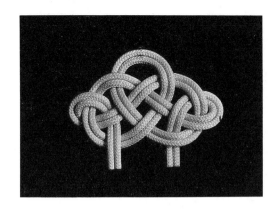

The Half-Hitched Carrick Bend

This ornamental Carrick Bend design is started by first forming the Unlocked Carrick Bend (see page 34), and pinning it to the working surface as shown in Figure 1. The remainder of the weave is made by following the illustrations. The completed knot is shown in Figure 9.

The design can be used in either the single form, above left, or the doubled form as shown above right. The doubled knot measures 9 inches wide and 7 inches high. The material required is two pieces of rope, one 5 feet long, the other 5½ feet long, and ½ inch in diameter. The longer of the two ropes is used for the outside of the knot.

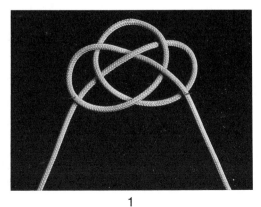

1

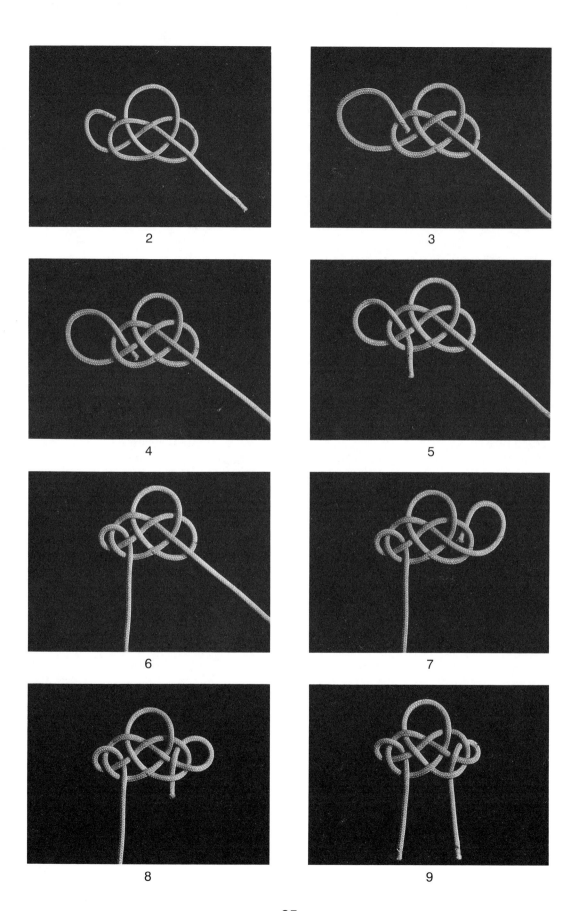

2

3

4

5

6

7

8

9

The Lark's Head Carrick Bend

This weave is used principally as wearing apparel ornamentation, or it can be worn as a choker around the neck or as a bracelet. It takes its name from the Lark's Head type knot woven into each side of the design.

It is made by first forming the two-strand Carrick Bend weave (see page 39). However, the ends should appear as shown on page 67, Figure 1. The Lark's Head knots are now added to the design as shown in Figures 2 through 8 to complete the knot.

The design illustrated above, when made to wear as a choker, requires two pieces of 1/8-inch-diameter cord, each 3 feet long. It measures 3 1/2 inches wide and 1 inch high. The amount of material indicated will allow sufficient material to tie the design around the neck.

This design, when used as a wall ornament, can be made from two pieces of 1/4-inch-diameter rope, each 3 feet long. It measures 10 inches wide and 2 inches high.

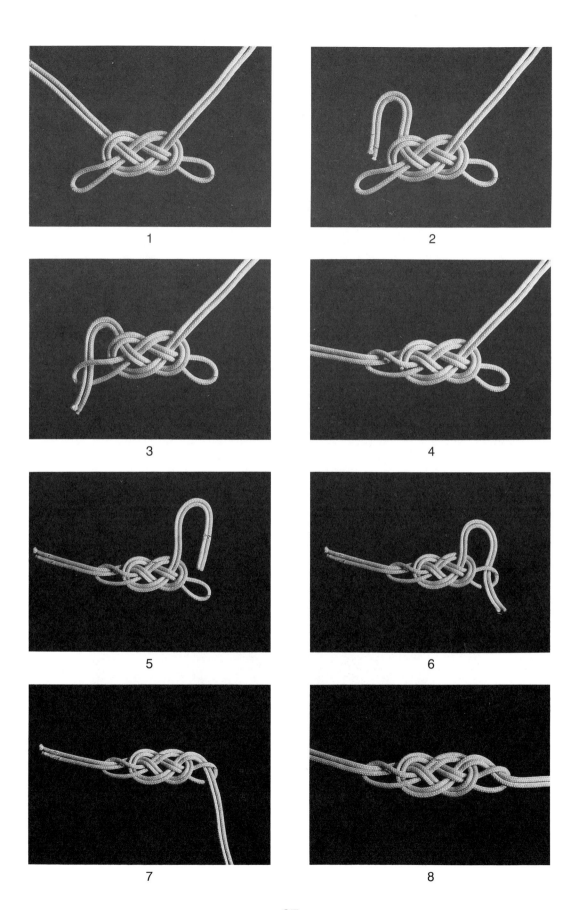

1

2

3

4

5

6

7

8

The Carrick Bend Coaster

This small mat or coaster is made by first forming the Carrick Bend on a Bight as illustrated on page 31, and then pinning it to the working surface as shown in Figure 1. Note that one end has been left much longer. The reason for this is that many designs are made from a single piece of rope. The process of doubling is done by first completing the basic design and then duplicating the original weave by doubling it with the long end. The doubling process starts in Figure 2 and continues step by step until completed (Figure 18).

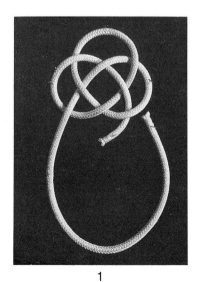

1

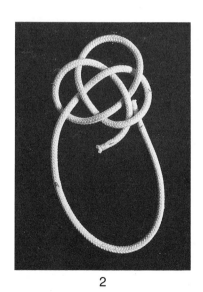

2

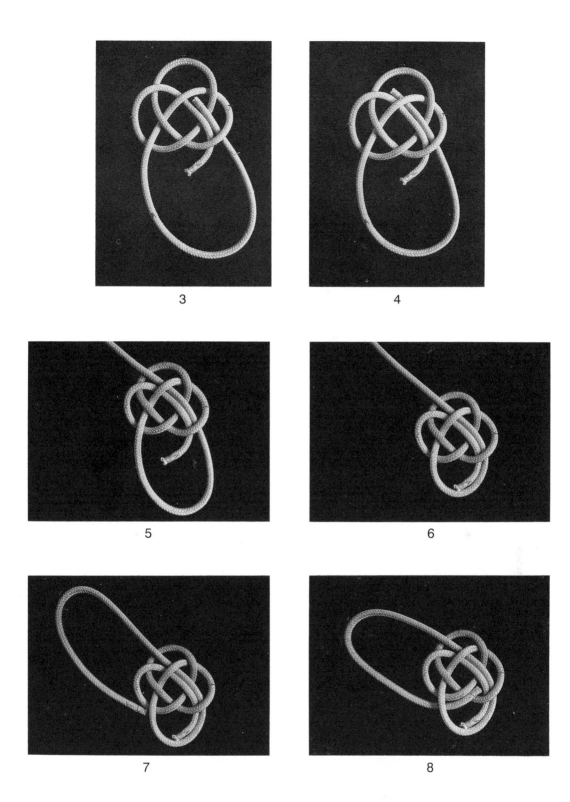

3

4

5

6

7

8

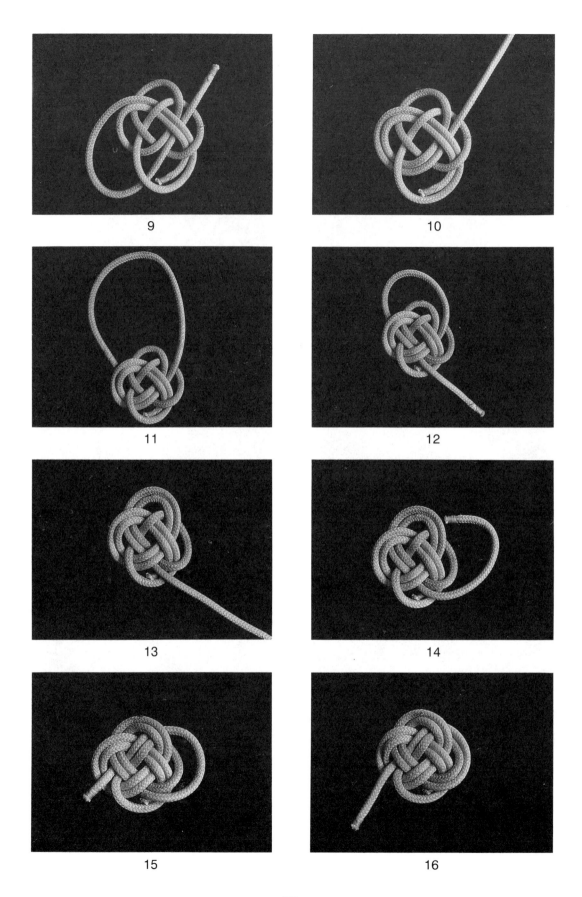

9

10

11

12

13

14

15

16

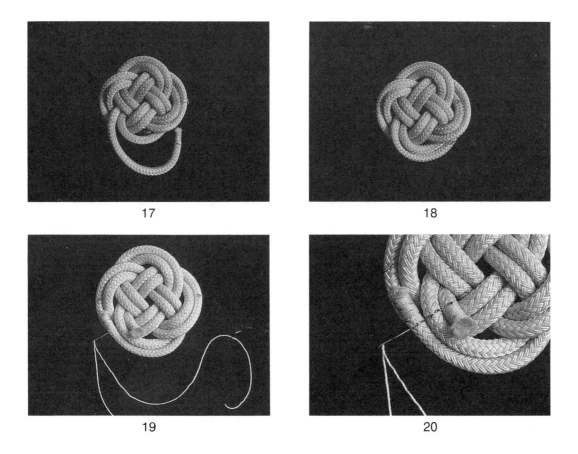

17

18

19

20

How to Conceal and Fasten the Ends

When the design has been completely woven, pulled up, and blocked as in Figure 18, the next problem is to fasten and conceal the ends. This is done by turning the design over so it appears as shown in Figure 19. Note that when the doubling procedure has been completed, both rope ends should finish up next to each other. Take a needle and strong thread and push the needle through the loose end on the left, continue through the solid center strand, and finally through the other loose end on the right. This is shown in more detail in Figure 20. The thread is now pulled through the rope and the same procedure is followed several more times. Knot the thread, cut off the ends of the rope close, and it is finished. The coasters can either be left in their natural rope finish or they can be painted with several coats of paint or shellac.

The design illustrated in Figure 18 is 4 inches in diameter. It was made with one piece of $1/4$-inch-diameter rope, 5 feet long.

The Side Interlocking Carrick Bend

This design is started from the left end using one piece of rope as illustrated in Figure 1. It is important to note at this point that the left-hand side of the weave is locked and the right-hand side is unlocked. Please refer to page 72, Figure 1.

In making this type of weave there are many points that are in the unlocked position, as can be seen in Figure 2. The locking process begins in Figure 3 for the first Carrick Bend and for the second one in Figure 4 as the weave is continued. Note, however, that the second Carrick Bend is left in a partially unlocked condition (Figure 5). This procedure is followed throughout the weaving operation. It is not changed until the last knot required has been formed, which is then locked as shown in Figure 10.

The completed designs, pulled up and blocked, are shown above. The one on the left is made with a single rope and the one on the right with a doubled rope.

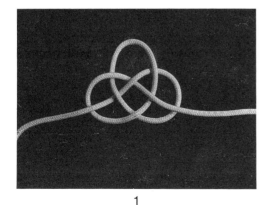

1

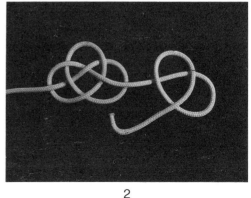

2

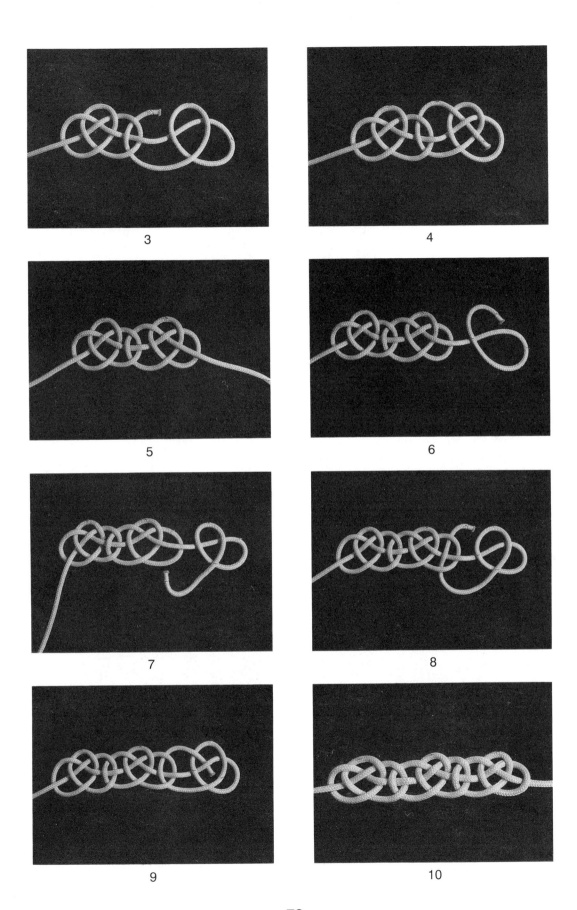

3

4

5

6

7

8

9

10

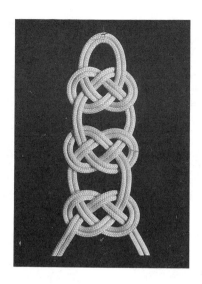

The Doubled Carrick Bend Chain

This design is a series of Carrick Bends woven end on end. The pattern is started as shown on page 33. It is pinned to the working surface as shown in Figure 1.

Note: This pattern is made of left and right Carrick Bends. Examine the loop in Figure 2 and compare it with the loop in Figure 6. You will see that in Figure 2 the working cord goes over and in Figure 6 the working cord goes under. The completed figure, pulled up and blocked, is shown in Figure 8.

The above design is 6 inches wide and 18 inches high. The material required is one piece of rope 9 feet long and one piece 8 feet long, 3⁄8 inch in diameter. A smaller design can be made by using smaller cordage.

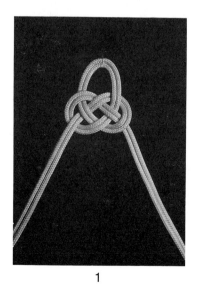

1

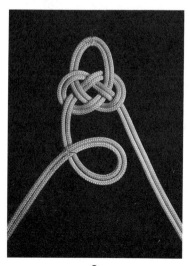

2

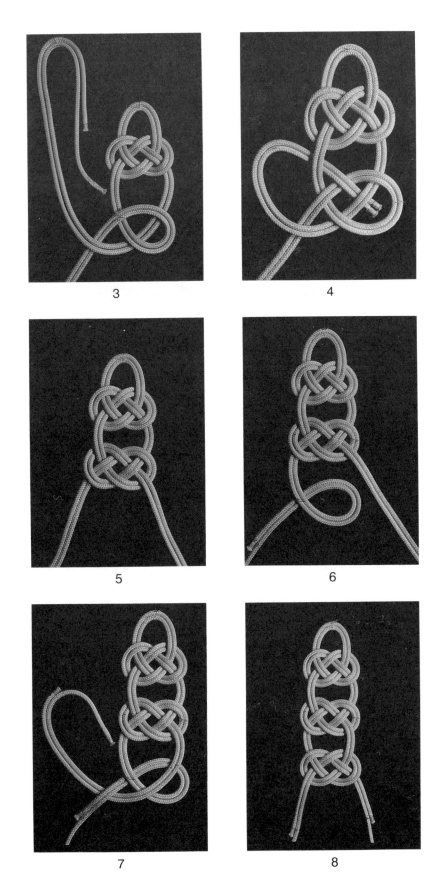

3

4

5

6

7

8

Carrick Bend Wreath Design

This design is formed using a series of Carrick Bends woven edge to edge. The knot used in this manner will yield many different ways to display the figure. It can be used just as it is shown here, as a wall hanging, or as a frame for a picture.

The design is started by first forming the Doubled Carrick Bend on a Bight and then pinning it to the working surface as illustrated in Figure 1. The manner of forming this knot is shown on page 33. Next, proceed to weave the second Carrick Bend with the left-hand ropes (Figures 2-6). This is followed by weaving the third Carrick Bend on the right-hand side (Figures 6-10). Please turn to page 79, where the method of completing this design is described.

The above design is 10 inches wide and 12 inches high. The material required is two pieces of rope, one 8 feet long and the other 9 feet long, 3/8 inch in diameter. The longer of the ropes is used on the outside edge of the weave.

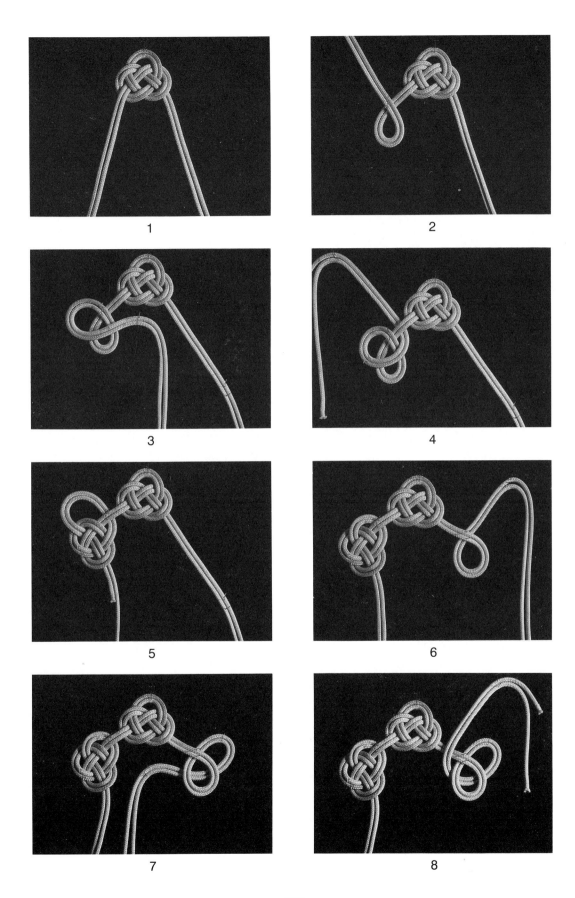

1

2

3

4

5

6

7

8

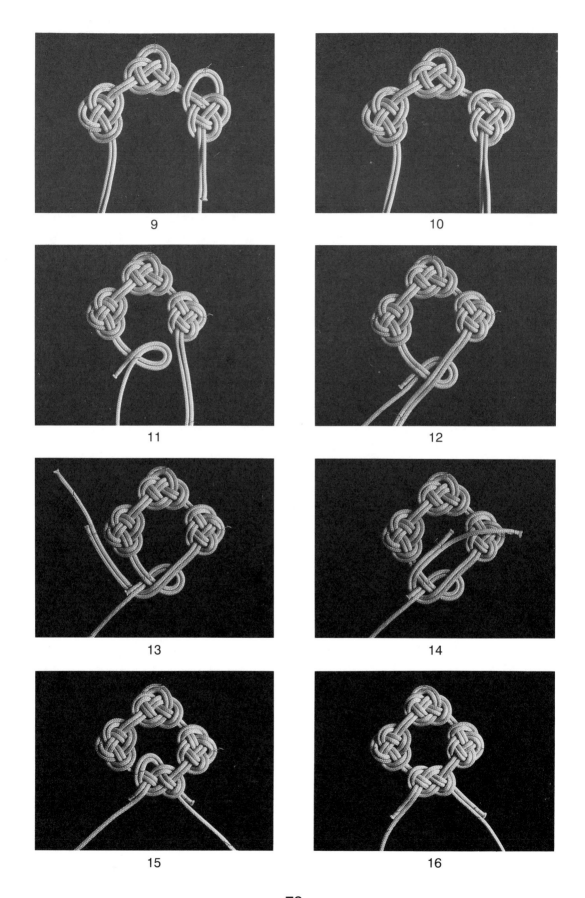

9

10

11

12

13

14

15

16

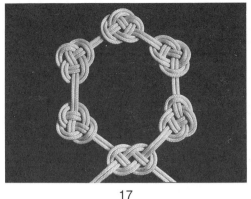

17

18

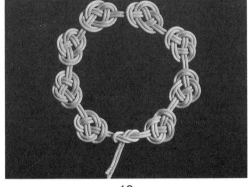

19

To finish the design, the ropes on the left are pinned in the position shown in Figure 11. Next, pick up the ropes on the right and weave them through the left group as shown in Figures 12 through 15. The completed design, pulled up and blocked, is illustrated in Figure 16.

Different patterns can be formed using the same procedure, such as those illustrated in Figures 17, 18, and 19, the only difference being in the spacing and number of Carrick Bends used.

Another variation can be made by using either three ropes of the same color or three cords of different colors.

Note that the wreath designs in Figures 17 and 18 were made with left and right Carrick Bends and Figure 19 was made with only right-hand Carrick Bends.

Figure 17 is 12 inches wide, and requires two pieces, each 12 feet long. Figure 18 is 10 inches wide, and requires two pieces, each 11 feet long. Figure 19 is 14 inches wide, and requires two pieces, each 18 feet long.

All designs were made with 1/4-inch-diameter rope.

The Epaulet Carrick Bend

This weave is frequently used as a decorative shoulder braid on uniforms and is called an epaulet.

It is made by first forming the Locked Carrick Bend as illustrated on page 29, and pinning it to the working surface in a slightly opened position (Figure 1). The weaving process is now continued (Figures 2-7). The completed design (after doubling) is shown in Figure 8 before the ends have been sewn together and cut off. The sewing operation is described on page 71.

The knot as illustrated above is 7 inches wide and 2½ inches high. The material required is two pieces of rope, each 3½ feet long and ¼ inch in diameter.

This knot is extremely attractive when made in small colored cord and makes an excellent accent knot to be displayed along with a larger weave.

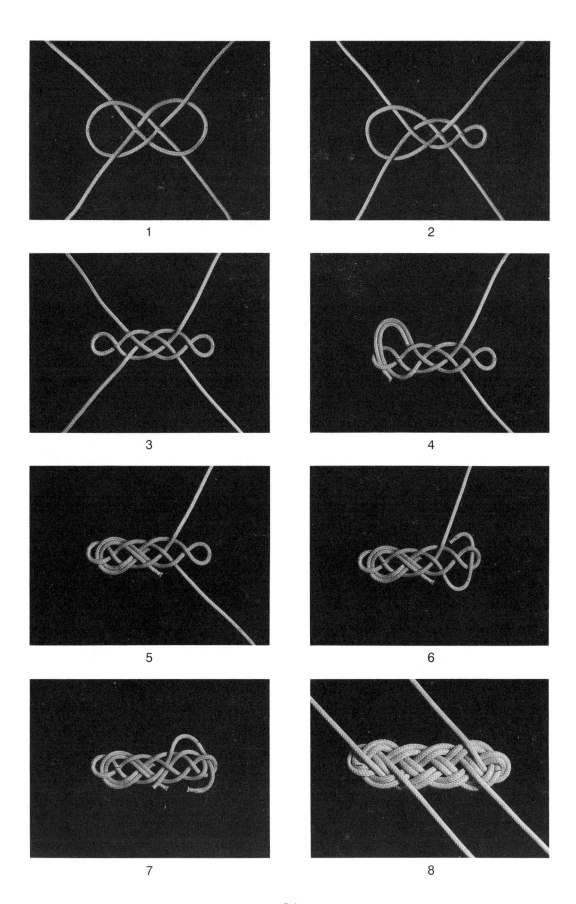

The Hanging Epaulet Weave

This design is similar to that shown on page 80, but is used only for hanging ornaments. It can also be formed with large rope and used individually as a wall display.

The doubled knot above right measures 7½ inches wide by 3 inches high. It was made with four pieces of rope, each ¼ inch in diameter and 30 inches long.

The design is started by forming the Unlocked Carrick Bend, which is then pinned to the working surface as in Figure 1. At this point additional slack is pulled into the right- and left-hand loops (Figure 2). This provides enough slack to form the twisted loops shown in Figures 3 and 4. The weaving operation is now performed (Figures 5-7) and the completed design, pulled up and blocked, appears in Figure 8.

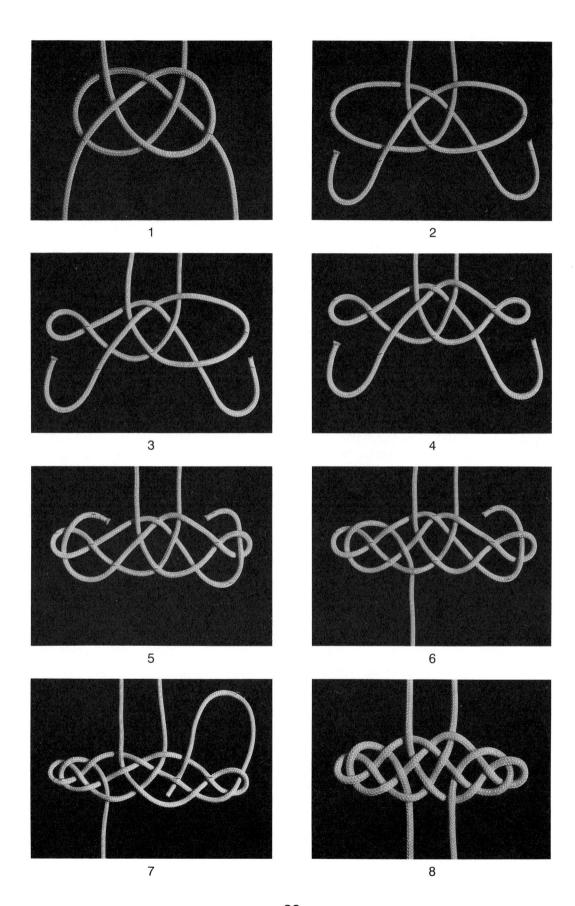

 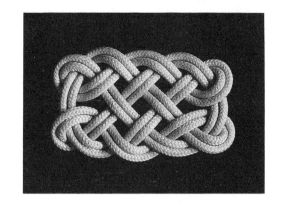

The Twin Half-Hitched Carrick Bend Weave

For a larger coaster, a table hot pad, or a small ornamental mat, this design has proven successful.

It is started with the Unlocked Carrick Bend formed as shown on page 35 and pinned to the working surface as shown in Figure 1. The weave is continued as illustrated in Figures 2 through 5. The completed weave is shown in Figure 6. Made in this manner it can be used either singly, or doubled as part of a wall hanging. If a mat design is required, then proceed to double the knot (Figures 7 and 8). When the weaving process has been completed, the ends of the rope should be sewn together as shown on page 71, Figure 19.

The design illustrated, above right, is 6½ inches wide and 3½ inches high. The material required is two pieces of rope ¼ inch in diameter, each 6 feet long. The single design, above left, requires two pieces of rope, each 3 feet long.

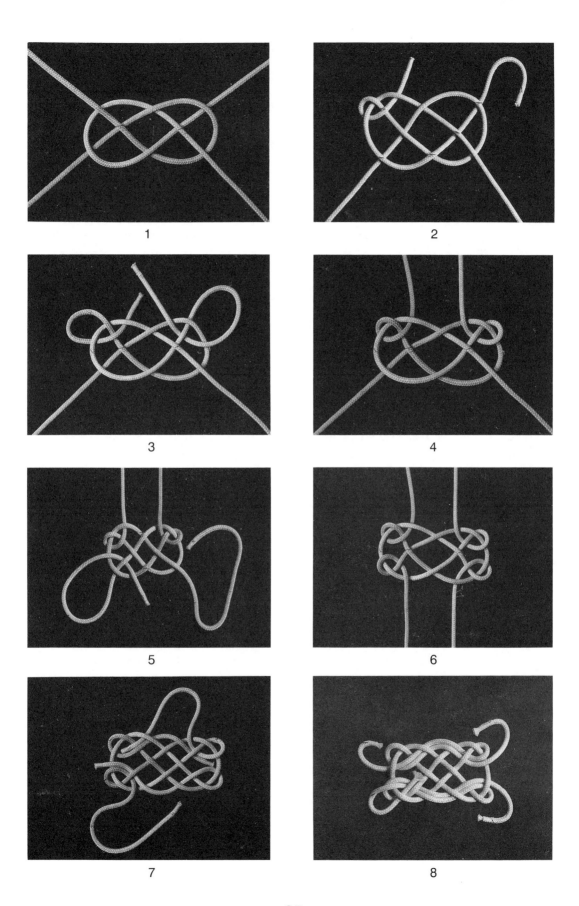

1

2

3

4

5

6

7

8

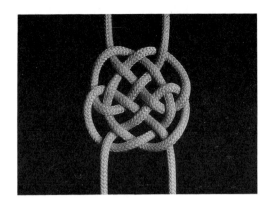 

The End Interlocking Carrick Bend

The design is actually two Unlocked Carrick Bends with their ends interwoven to interlock both knots, resulting in one woven pattern. The weave is started with the Unlocked Carrick Bend on page 35, and is pinned to the working surface as shown in Figure 1. Begin the weave with the left-hand end (Figure 2). Then proceed to weave with the right-hand end (Figures 4-7). The completed knot, pulled up and blocked, is shown in Figure 8.

The above design on the right is 7 inches high and 5 inches wide. The material required is four pieces of rope ¼ inch in diameter, each 42 inches long.

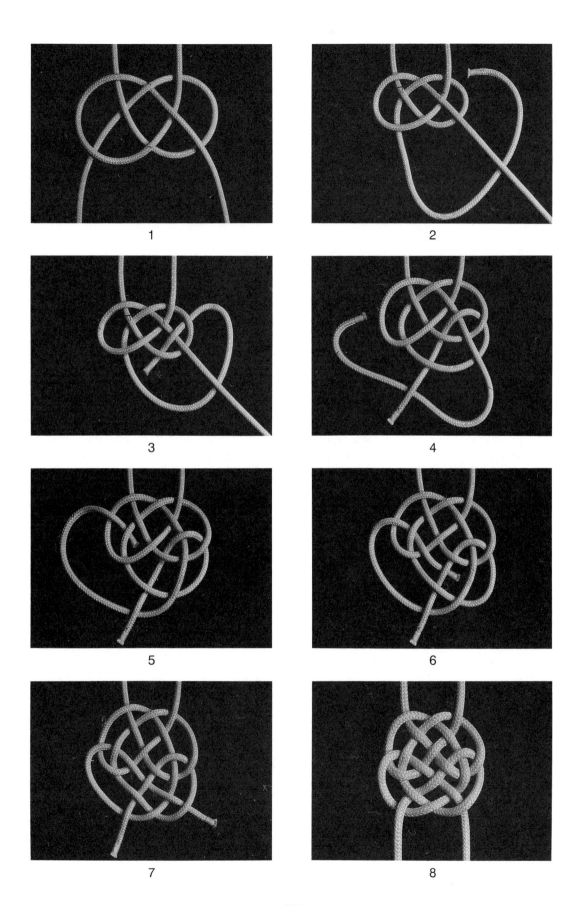

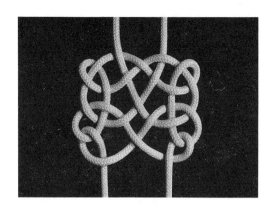 

The Hitched Carrick Bend Weave

This weave is started by first forming the Unlocked Carrick Bend as illustrated in Figure 1.

Note: At this point, refer to page 19, Figures 3 and 4, for a caution.

The weave is now continued using both the left and right cords (Figures 2-9). The completed knot pulled up and blocked is shown in Figure 10.

This design can be made either singly or doubled as shown above. The doubled weave requires four pieces of rope, 1/4 inch in diameter, each 4 feet long. It measures 7 inches wide and 8 inches high.

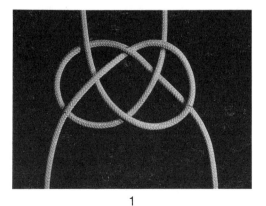 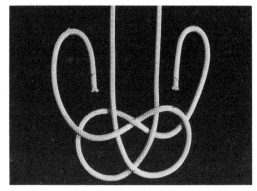

1

2

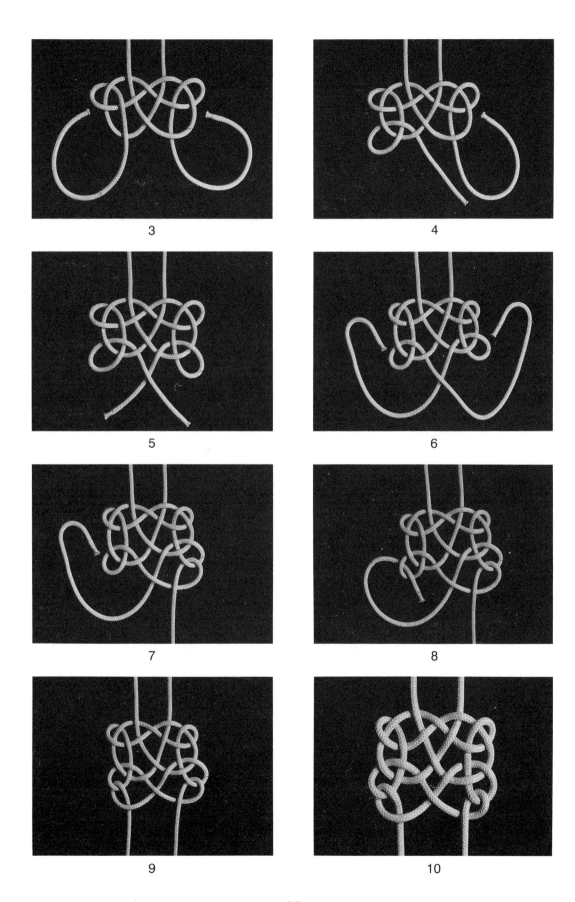

3

4

5

6

7

8

9

10

The Flemish Carrick Bend

This very attractive design is started with the Locked Carrick Bend, as illustrated on page 29, and pinned to the working surface as shown in Figure 1. The remainder of the weave is made as shown in Figures 2 through 7. The completed design, pulled up and blocked (see page 20) is illustrated in Figure 8.

The doubled knot, above right, measures 6½ inches wide and 8 inches high. The material required is four pieces of rope, each ¼ inch in diameter and 4 feet long.

This knot can also be started from a Carrick Bend on a Bight (see page 31). It forms a very decorative wall hanging.

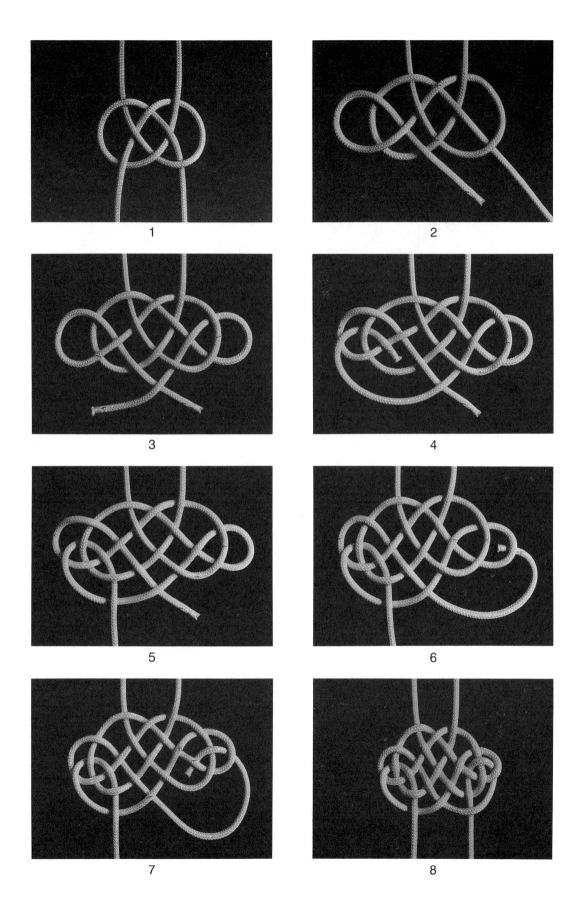

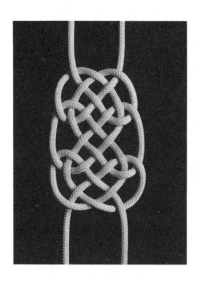 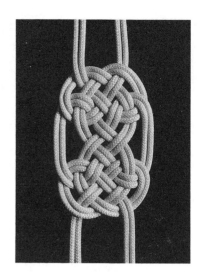

The Four-Strand Sennit Carrick Bend

This design takes its name from the weave joining the upper and lower Carrick Bends that resembles the Four-Strand Sennit Weave.

The weave is started by forming the Unlocked Carrick Bend, which is pinned to the working surface as shown in Figure 1. The design is continued, crossing the left- and right-hand ends (Figure 2). Continue to weave the left-hand end (Figures 3-4) and follow by weaving the right-hand end (Figures 5-6).

The weave is continued on pages 94 and 95, Figures 7 through 13, and the completed design, pulled up and blocked, is illustrated in Figure 14.

The doubled knot pictured above right measures 5 inches wide and 11 inches high. The material required is four pieces of ¼-inch-diameter rope, each 6 feet long.

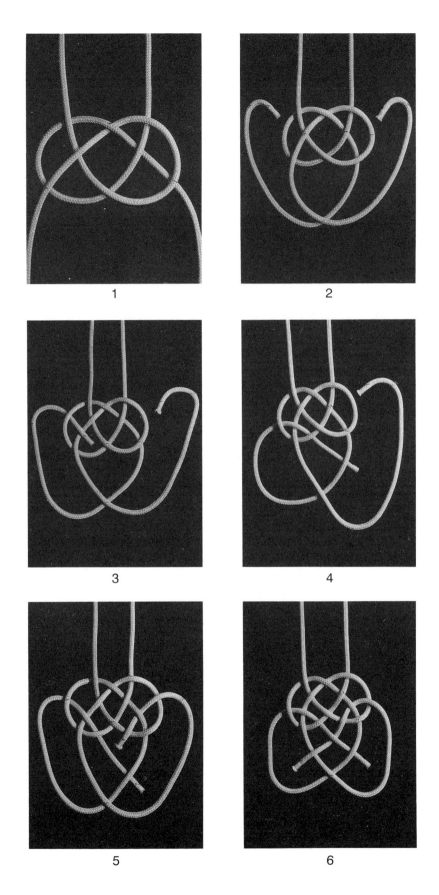

1

2

3

4

5

6

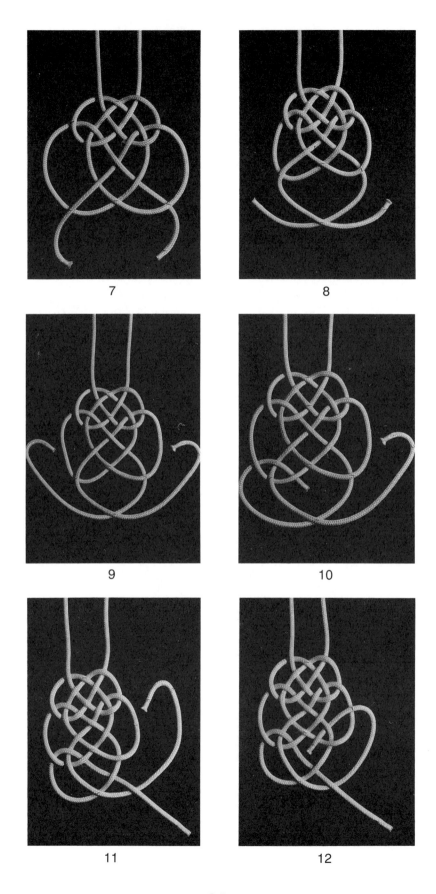

7

8

9

10

11

12

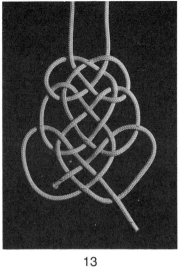

13

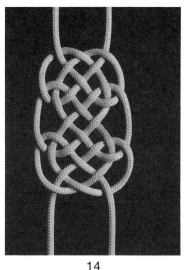

14

The above design can also be started from an Unlocked Carrick Bend on a Bight (see page 34). It will then appear as illustrated in Figure 15, and can be used as a wall hanging, or a mat when doubled (Figure 16).

The design shown in Figure 14 can also be made by using six pieces of rope in two groups of three each, which will yield a triple-strand design. This may be further varied by using two or three different colored ropes on each side.

The mat design in Figure 16 measures 5 inches wide and 8 inches high. The material required is one piece of ¼-inch-diameter rope, 14 feet long.

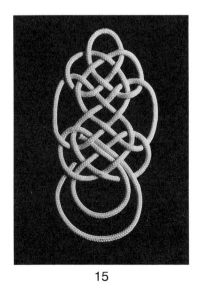

15

16

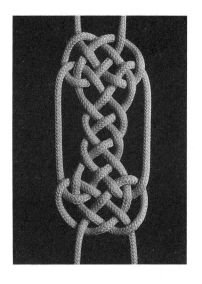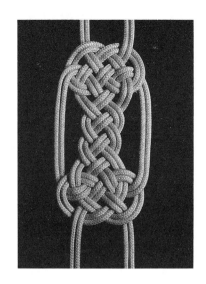

The Long Four-Strand Sennit Carrick Bend

This knot is very much like that pictured on page 92. However, there is a slight difference in the manner in which it is made. It will be noted that the Four-Strand Sennit Weave is much more pronounced and gives a pleasing effect to the knot.

Start the knot by forming the Unlocked Carrick Bend (see page 35), pinning it to the working surface as shown in Figure 1. The next step is quite important in order to tie the knot properly. The two ends of rope must be crossed over twice (Figure 2) and pinned in place. (It should be remembered at this point that the ends shown in these figures are much shorter than you will be using in the actual work. This is done to make the weaving details clearer.) The re-

mainder of the knot is made by first weaving a small portion with the right-hand rope and then a small portion with the left-hand rope (Figures 3-13). The completed design is shown in Figure 14, after it has been pulled up and blocked (see page 20).

The same design, tripled (filled out with two additional passes of rope), is illustrated in Figure 15, in a horizontal position. When the design is mounted on a piece of driftwood in this manner, and hung on a wall, it will become one of your favorite conversation pieces.

The doubled design shown above right measures 5½ inches wide and 13 inches high. The material required is four strands of ¼-inch-diameter rope, two 6 feet and two 7 feet long.

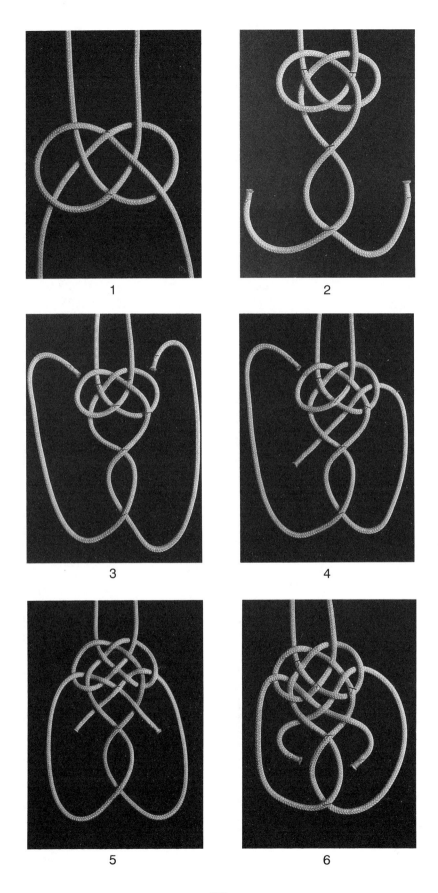

1

2

3

4

5

6

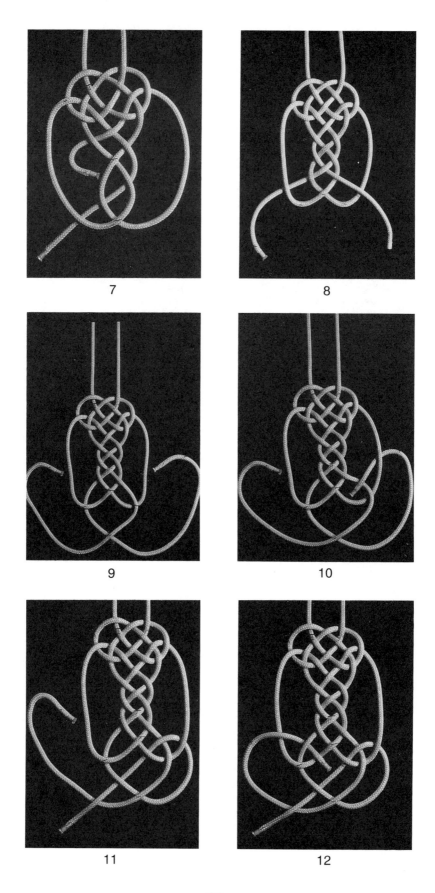

7

8

9

10

11

12

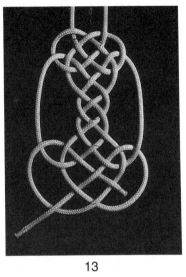

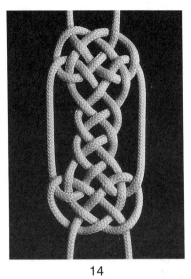

13

14

15

The Outside Pretzel Carrick Bend Weave

This design takes its name from the Pretzel Weave forming each side.

To start the knot, form the Unlocked Carrick Bend as shown on page 34, which is then pinned to the working surface as shown in Figure 1. Next, weave the left-hand pretzel, followed by the right-hand pretzel (Figures 2-4). The remainder of the knot is then tied by weaving the right-hand side rope through the left side, and finished by weaving the left-hand end through the right side. The completed design is shown in Figure 8.

The doubled knot weave pictured above right measures 6 inches wide and 9 inches high. The material required is four pieces of 1/4-inch-diameter rope, two 4 1/2 feet and two 5 1/2 feet long.

This knot can also be made by starting from a Carrick Bend on a Bight (see page 34), and can be used as a wall hanging by leaving the ends hanging as shown above right. It can also be made into a mat by weaving the design with single strands as shown, and doubling the knot with the ends as described on page 107.

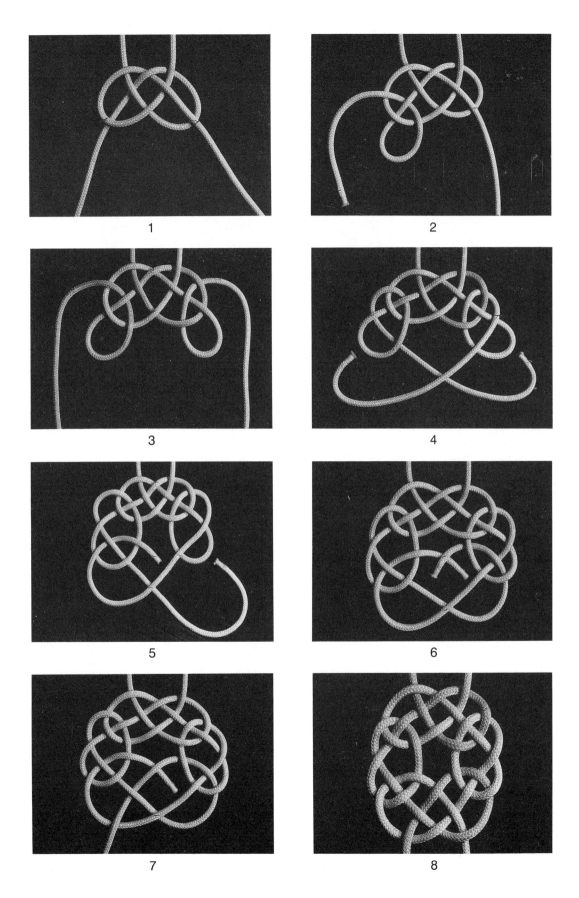

1

2

3

4

5

6

7

8

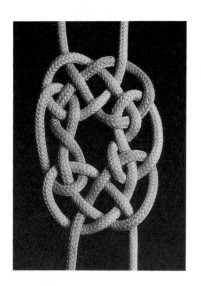 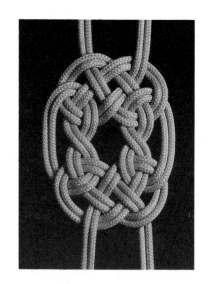

The Inside Pretzel Carrick Bend Weave

This weave resembles that illustrated on page 100, except the Pretzel Weave on each side is reversed.

The design is started by first forming the Unlocked Carrick Bend (see page 34), and pinning it to the working surface as shown in Figure 1. The weaving operation is performed by alternately forming a portion of the design on the left side and then a portion on the right side (Figures 2-7). The finished design is pictured in Figure 8, after being pulled up and blocked (see page 20).

The doubled knot, above right, measures 5 inches wide and 10 inches high. Material required is four pieces of rope ¼ inch in diameter, two 4½ feet and two 5½ feet long.

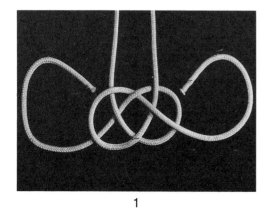

1

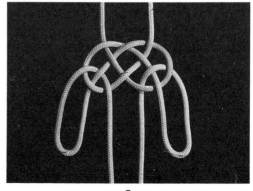

2

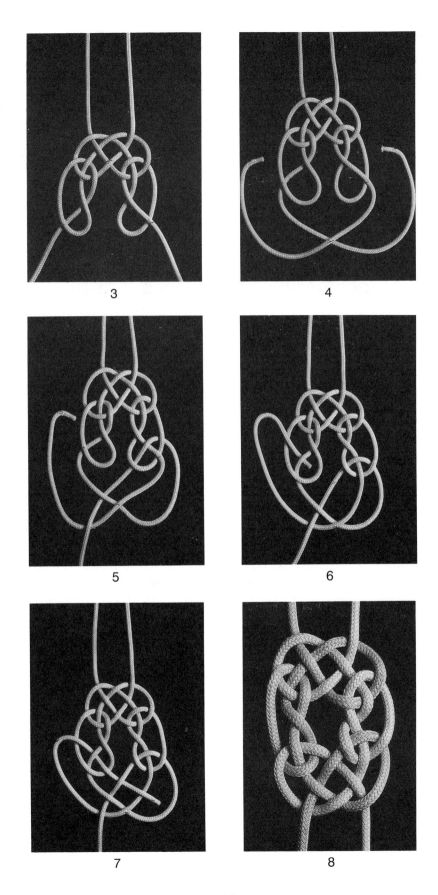

3

4

5

6

7

8

 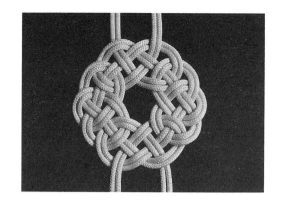

Interlocking Carrick Bend Wreath

This weave is generally used as part of a wall hanging. However, it makes a very attractive wall display and can be woven using colored rope combinations. It may also be used as a tabletop decoration or centerpiece. The boatman can use it as a cushion for a deck block by first making the weave, then fastening it to the deck with brass brads, and finally shackling the block to the deck pad.

The doubled design above right measures 7 inches in diameter. The material required is four pieces of rope, each 4 feet long and ¼ inch in diameter.

The weave is started by forming an Unlocked Carrick Bend, as shown on page 34, and pinning it to the work surface as illustrated in Figure 1. At this point, weave with the left-hand rope only, complete the figure, shown on the left-hand side in Figures 2 through 6, and pin in place. Go back to Figure 2 and repeat the right-hand weave with the right-hand rope until you reach Figure 6, and pin in place. At this point the left and right sides of the weave are joined with the final Carrick Bend. This is started as illustrated in Figure 7. The wreath is now completed by weaving with both cords (Figures 8-11), rather than with a single end as previously. The completed design is shown in Figure 12 after being pulled up and blocked.

To keep the proper shape when weaving such a design, you should pin the work constantly as it progresses.

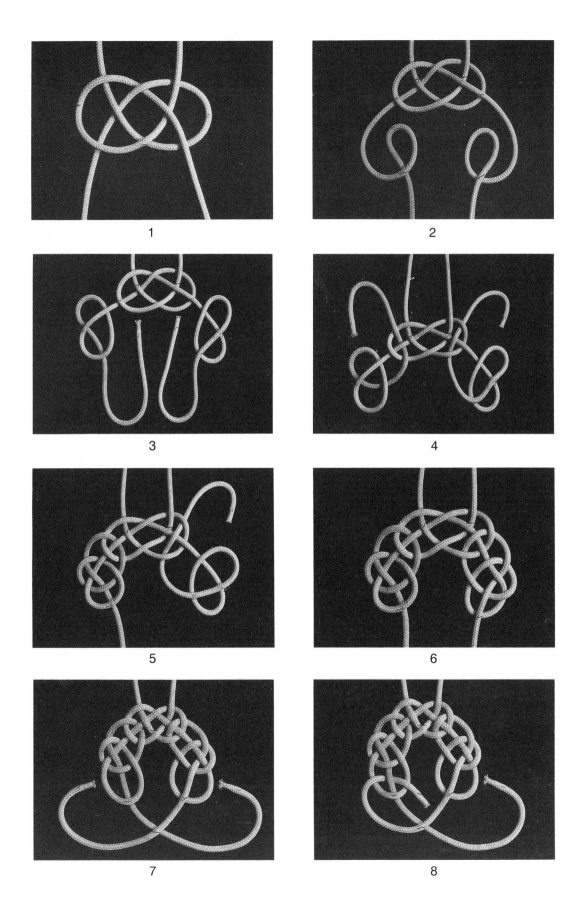

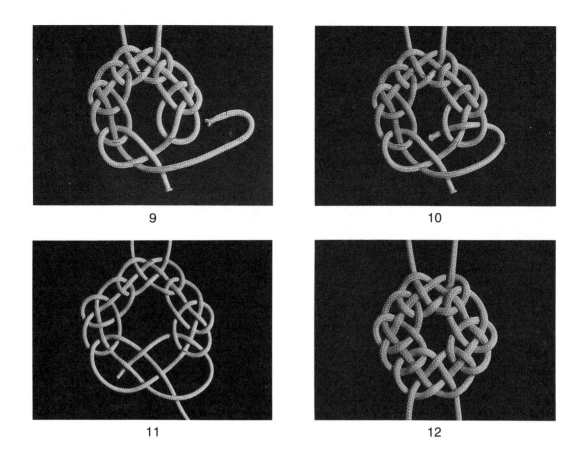

9

10

11

12

The wreath illustrated above can be varied in appearance by forming the same design and using different color combinations in the rope material, as shown in Figure 13.

The design can also be modified by repeating the weaves shown in Figures 2 through 6 and adding additional Carrick Bends. The design will then appear as illustrated in Figure 14.

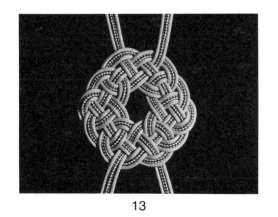

13

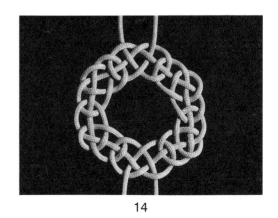

14

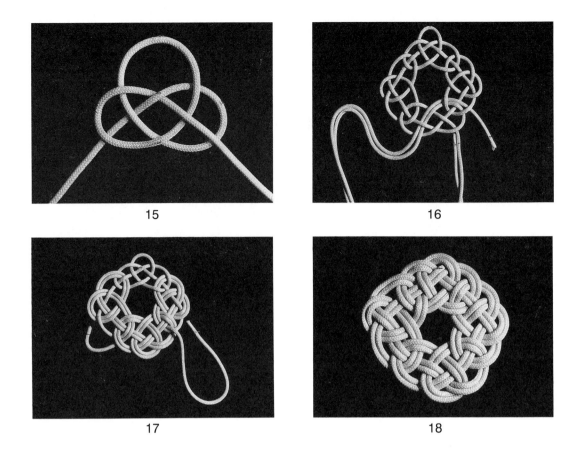

15

16

17

18

In order to make an Interlocking Carrick Bend Wreath mat, start from a bight, as illustrated in Figure 15, rather than with two ends (Figure 1).

To form this design, make an Unlocked Carrick Bend on a Bight (see page 34), and pin it to the working surface as illustrated in Figure 15. Now go back to Figure 2 and proceed in the same manner until the design has been completed (Figure 12). The next step is the doubling operation, which is started as shown in

Figure 16. Figure 17 shows how the weave appears when the doubling operation has been half completed. After the doubling has been completed, the weave is pulled up and blocked and the ends sewn and cut off as illustrated on page 71. The completed design is illustrated in Figure 18. It measures 8 inches in diameter and was made from one piece of rope ¼ inch in diameter and 18 feet long.

The Royal Carrick Bend

This is a very handsome and ornamental variation of the Carrick Bend. It can done quite rapidly and, when made with large rope, makes an attractive wall hanging.

The design is started by first making an Unlocked Carrick Bend (see page 34), and pinning it to the working surface as shown in Figure 1. The weave is then continued using both the left and right ropes (Figures 2-10). The completed basic weave is shown in Figure 14 on page 110. Now the doubling process is done as explained on page 68.

The design illustrated above is 7 inches wide and 5½ inches high. The material required is one piece of rope, 18 feet long and ¼ inch in diameter.

Note: This weave will be in an unlocked condition at many points while it is being made. Therefore it is important that the knot be well pinned as you work.

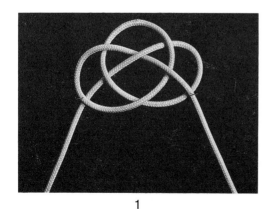

1

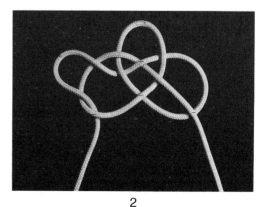

2

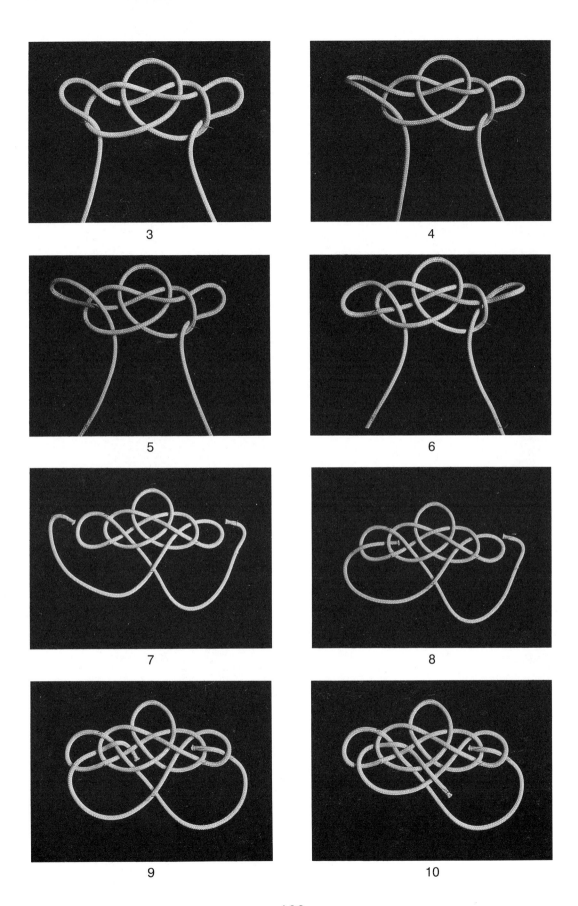

3

4

5

6

7

8

9

10

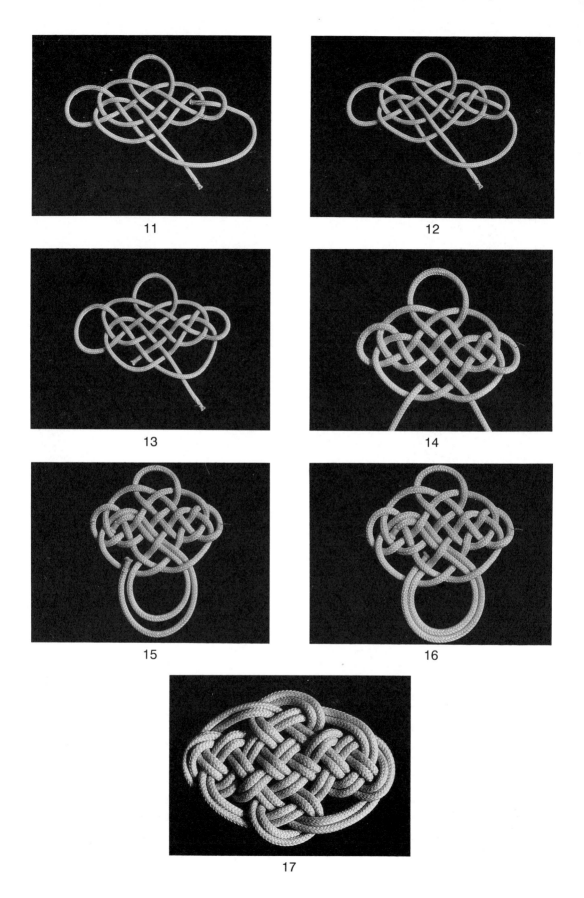

11

12

13

14

15

16

17

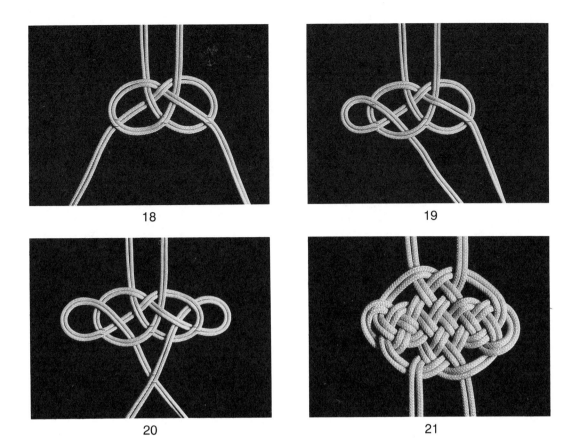

18

19

20

21

The Royal Carrick Bend can also be fashioned into a wall hanging such as is illustrated in Figure 21.

Rather than the weave being started from a bight as shown in Figure 1, this design is started by pinning two sets of two pieces of rope to the working surface in the form of the Unlocked Carrick Bend (Figure 18). The partially com-pleted figure is illustrated in Figures 19 and 20. To finish the knot, turn to page 109, Figure 7, and continue to weave until Figure 14 on page 110 is reached. This completes the design, which is woven with doubled ropes rather than single. The completed design is shown in Figure 21, after being pulled up and blocked.

The Short and Long Carrick Bend Mats

This is one of the most interesting designs that can be made from the basic Carrick Bend knot. It is not only decorative, but quite functional as well. It can be used as a hot pad, table decoration, or floor mat.

A decorative wall hanging such as that shown at the top left measures 13 inches wide and 6 inches high. To make it requires 20 feet of ½-inch-diameter rope. The triple-strand weave shown above right measures 16 inches wide and 7½ inches high. The material required is 35 feet of ½-inch rope.

To start, make a locked Carrick Bend on a Bight as shown on page 31, which is then pinned to the work surface as shown in Figure 1. The weave is continued until complete (Figure 12). At this point, start to double the design (Figure 13). The finished weave is shown in Figure 14. The ends are sewn and cut off as shown on page 71.

The mat can be made longer by simply starting at the point illustrated on page 114 (Figure 12), pulling some slack in the loops (Figures 15-16), and continuing the weave (Figures 17-18). The doubling process is now performed (Figure 13), and the half-completed weave is shown in Figure 19. The ends are sewn and cut off. The finished mat is shown in Figure 20.

A very attractive floor mat can be made by using manila rope or braided Dacron or nylon rope. In order to have it large enough, it should be made with five passes rather than two as illustrated in Figure 14 or Figure 20. This, of course, requires more rope. (See page 149).

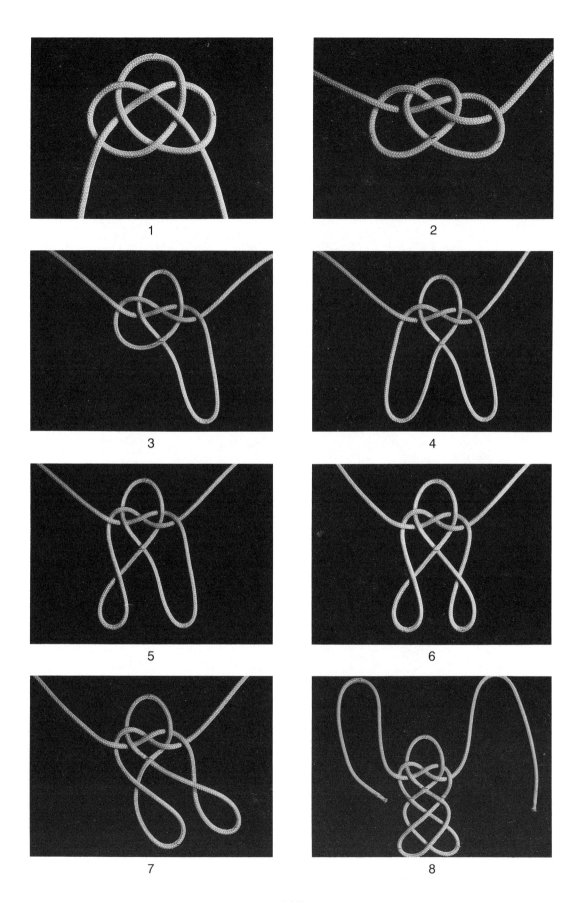

1

2

3

4

5

6

7

8

113

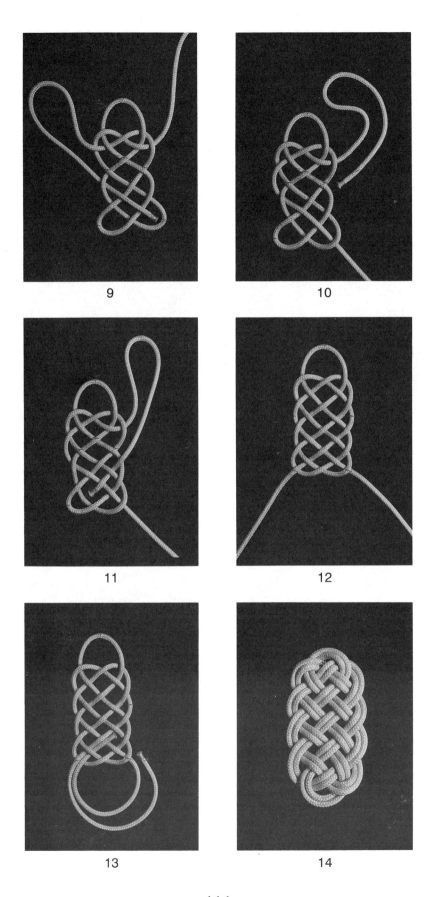

9

10

11

12

13

14

114

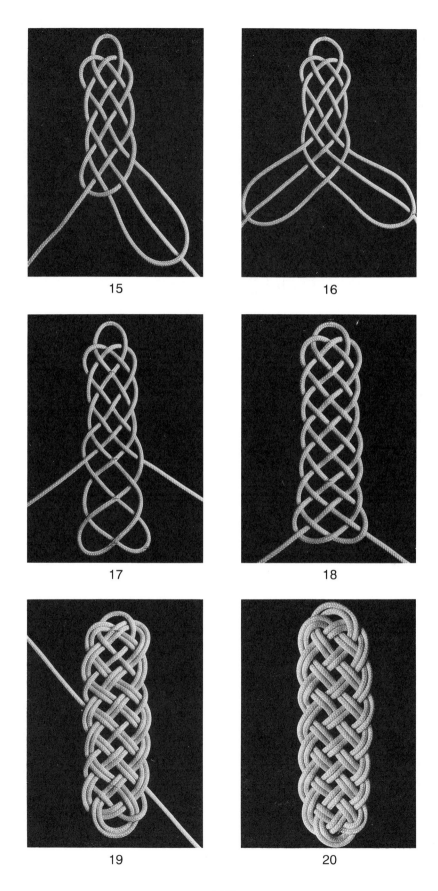

15

16

17

18

19

20

The Cross Weave

This knot is handsome in appearance and very simple to tie. Although it looks complicated, it requires only a few minutes to form.

It is started by pinning the first rope to the working surface as shown in Figure 1. The second rope is introduced to the design as shown in Figure 2 and the weave is then completed using the right-hand rope (Figures 3-9). The completed weave is shown pulled up and blocked in Figure 10.

This weave can also be made using one piece of rope, by doubling it over and pinning the center to the working surface. Start the weave with the left-hand rope and then the right-hand rope as shown in Figures 1 and 2.

The doubled design, above right, measures 5 inches wide and 7 inches high. Material is two pieces of ⅜-inch-diameter rope, each 40 inches long.

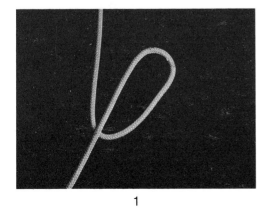

1

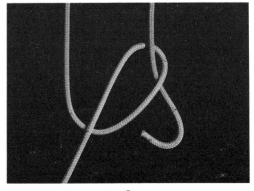

2

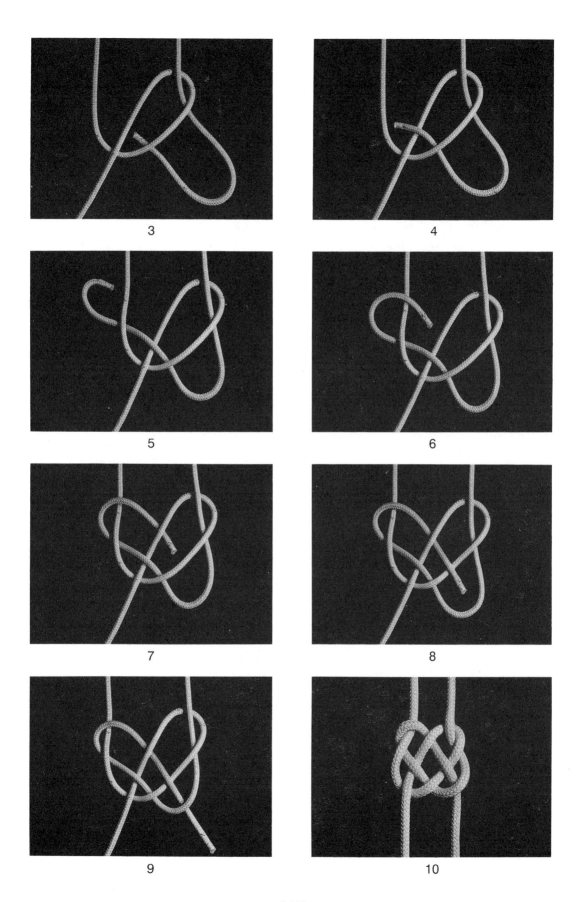

3

4

5

6

7

8

9

10

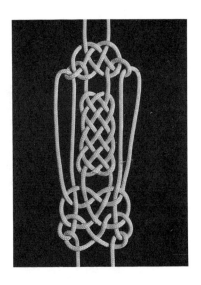 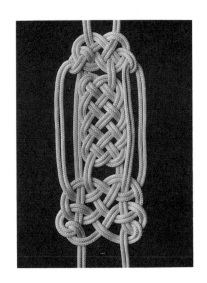

How to Combine Several Knots into a Wall Hanging

Many attractive wall hangings can be fashioned by combining any number of individual knots to form a large display. The method of doing this is illustrated in Figures 1 through 6. It must, of course, be remembered that the length of the design will be controlled by the amount of material you use to start it.

The figure above left measures 7 inches wide and 22 inches high. The material required is two pieces of rope, each 9 feet long and 1/4 inch in diameter. The figure above right has been doubled and requires four pieces of rope, two 10 feet and two 12 feet long.

The design is started by first forming the Half-Hitched Carrick Bend (see page 64), to which is added the Short Carrick Bend Mat weave (see page 112). Next, an Unlocked Carrick Bend is formed as in Figure 3 and the ends are pulled through the ears of the Half-Hitched Carrick Bend to form long loops (Figure 4). The remainder of the design is finished off as illustrated on page 89 (Figures 5-9).

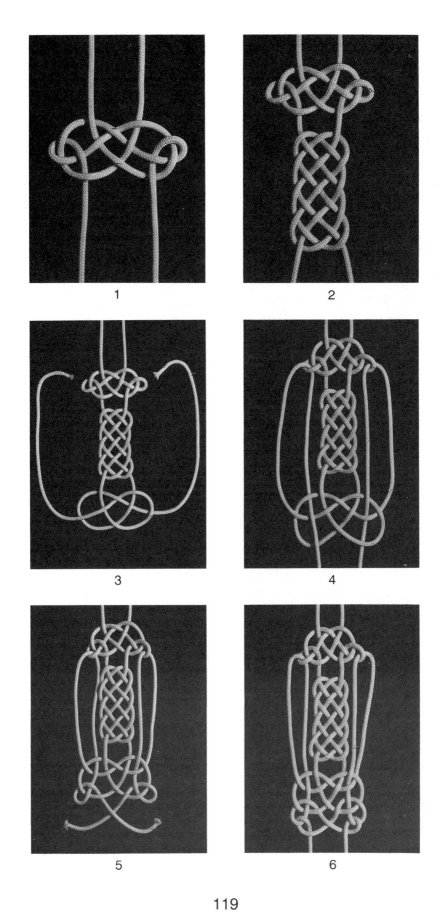

1

2

3

4

5

6

Grouped Tassels

Frequently you will want to finish off a wall hanging or a woman's belt with several tassels, as shown in the illustration at the left.

They are made one at a time (see page 58) and are adjusted up or down on the rope as required to have the top at the desired height.

When all of the tassels have been formed, then the bottoms should be trimmed. The tassels here have been trimmed to form two pairs. However, they can also be left untrimmed, or each one can be trimmed to a different length.

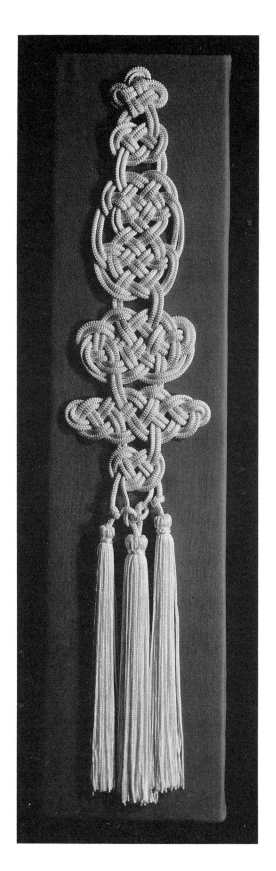

Small Oriental Wall Hangings

This design can be used as a bell cord or as an ornamental wall hanging.

The knots used to form the design are made one following the other as shown on page 118. The method of tying each one is shown on the following pages, starting from the top:

This design is mounted on a board 6 inches wide and 2 feet high. The material required is two pieces of $1/8$-inch-diameter rope, each 24 feet long. These are doubled over, forming two groups of two cords each, which are used to start the Dragonfly Knot from a bight.

Large Oriental Wall Hangings

The designs shown on page 123 are each mounted on a display board measuring 1 foot wide and 7 feet high. They are made by selecting any of the individual knot designs illustrated elsewhere in this book and combining them into a hanging as described on page 118.

The design on the left requires 144 feet of ⅜-inch-diameter rope: one piece 50 feet long, one piece 46 feet long, and twelve pieces 4 feet long. Each tassel is made with three pieces of the 4-foot-long ropes, which are unlaid as shown in the center of Figure 1. They are now gathered into a group as shown on the right side of Figure 1 and tied to one of the rope endings as shown on the right side of Figure 2. The tassel is formed in the same manner as that shown on page 58. The seizing is made with a yarn removed from one of the strands; this provides a tie of the same color. Figure 3 illustrates two completed tassels, the third and fourth are now formed on the remaining ends.

The design opposite right was made with two pieces of ¼-inch-diameter rope, one piece 48 feet long, the other 44 feet in length. The tassels were made with chainette material as shown on page 58. For additional details on their construction, see page 124.

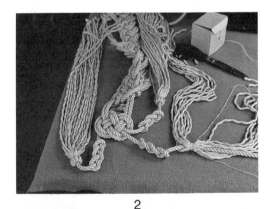

2

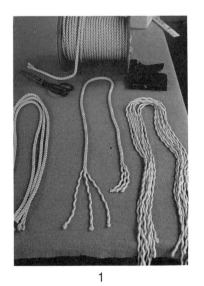

1

3

Construction of Oriental Wall Hanging

The hanging illustrated in Figure 1 is started with the Japanese Crown Knot (see page 54). This is followed by a Two-Strand Carrick Bend Weave as on page 38 (see note below). The next knot is made by forming two Doubled Carrick Bends on a Bight as shown on page 32, one with the left pair of ropes and another with the right pair. However, the last tuck should be left in the unlocked position and will appear as shown in Figure 6 on page 105. Next, pull some slack in each loop of the Carrick Bends, and cross them as shown in Figure 8 on page 113. The weave is now completed by following the steps shown in Figures 9 through 12 on page 114. The hanging is continued by forming the following designs:

The hanging shown in Figure 2 is started with the Dragonfly Knot illustrated on page 52 and the work is continued as follows:

The hanging is now finished off with a four-tassel group made with chainette as illustrated on page 58.

Note: Page 118 shows how several knots are combined in a series to form the hanging.

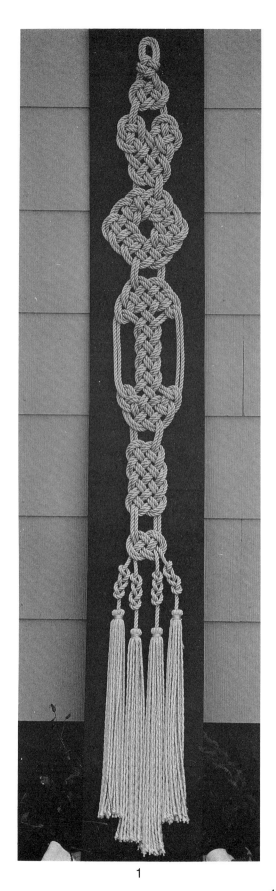 

1   2

Oriental Wall Hangings

A variety of wall ornaments can be fashioned by changing the knot combinations. This can be seen by comparing the designs on page 127 with those on page 125. Some of the knots that can be added to the hanging are illustrated on pages 128 and 129. In addition to different knots, it is also possible to create striking displays by using two different colored ropes, or, when working with three, using three different colors. The author has found that, when it is not possible to obtain colored rope, the design can be given any color desired by applying spray paint to the finished hanging.

The design illustrated in Figure 1 measures 7 inches wide and 5½ feet high. The material required is two pieces of ⅜-inch-diameter rope, one piece 36 feet long, the other 42 feet in length. (This hanging was made with blue nylon marine rope.) The knots used to form it are as follows, starting from the top (see page 118, which illustrates how to combine several knots to form a hanging):

(First make the Royal Carrick Bend and then trace the design by starting from the edge. See page 156, which illustrates how the tracing operation is done.)

The design is finished with a series of overhand knots.

The design illustrated in Figure 2 measures 7 inches wide and 4 feet high. The material required is two pieces of ⅜-inch-diameter rope, one 28 feet long, the other 32 feet long. (This design was made with blue nylon marine braided rope.) The hanging was started from the bottom and the knots used to form it are as follows, starting from the bottom:

The design is now finished off by forming a loop with one strand, tying it off with a seizing (see page 148, Figure 1, and page 61), and covering this with a Carrick Bend Turk's Head, page 56.

1

2

Weaves for Wall Hangings

The weaves shown in Figures 1 through 6 can be used as variations to replace any of those illustrated on pages 125 and 127, or they can be mounted as shown here, as separate individual hangings.

These knots can be formed by turning to the pages indicated after the figure numbers. All designs were made with 1/4-inch-diameter rope, and combined as illustrated on page 118.

Figure 1. See pages 38, 64, and 112. Design measures 5 inches wide and 22 inches high, and uses four pieces of material, two 9 feet and two 11 feet long.

Figure 2. See pages 38, 46, and 64. Design measures 7 inches wide and 9 inches high, and uses four pieces of material, each 7 feet long.

Figure 3. See pages 112 and 52. Design measures 3 inches wide and 20 inches high, and uses two pieces of material, one 20 feet and one 24 feet long.

Figure 4. See page 86. Design measures 5 inches wide and 22 inches high, and uses two pieces of material, one 24 feet and one 28 feet long.

Figure 5. See pages 64 and 96. Design measures 6 inches wide and 16 inches high, and uses two pieces of material, one 20 feet and one 22 feet long.

Figure 6. See pages 112, 104, and 102. Design measures 6 inches wide and 24 inches high, and uses two pieces of material, one 28 feet and one 32 feet long.

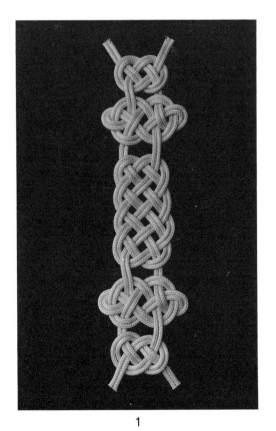

1

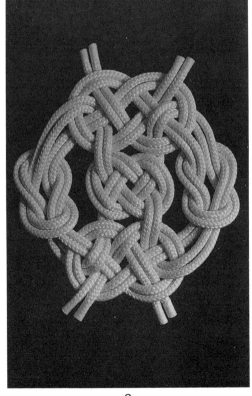

2

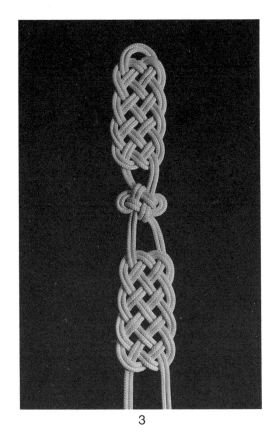

3

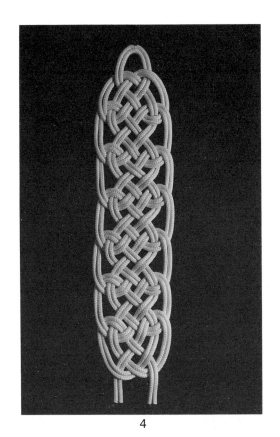

4

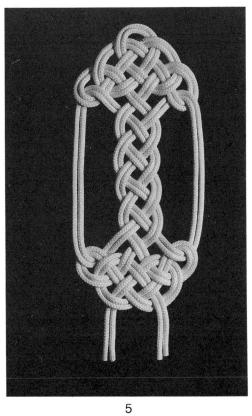

5

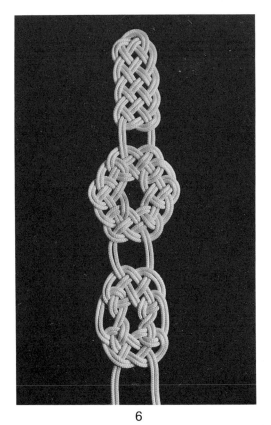

6

Women's Knotted Accessories

The designs illustrated in Figures 1, 2, 5, and 6 can be worn as chokers around the neck or as bracelets, when made of small cord (about 1/16 inch in diameter). When made with larger rope, say 1/8 inch or 1/4 inch diameter, they can be fashioned into attractive belts. The knots shown in these figures measure from 2 to 4 inches in length and were made with 1/16-inch-diameter material.

The pendants pictured in Figures 3 and 4 can be used as necklaces or the design in Figure 4 can be used as a shade pull when made with small cordage.

Methods of making the basic knots used in the examples are as follows:

Note: This design was made by using two pieces of doubled cord and starting the design from the center Carrick Bend and working both ways, right and left.

This necklace was made of two pieces of 1/16-inch-diameter cord, each 10 feet long.

This knot is formed by first making the Royal Carrick Bend, then "tracing"—see page 156, Figure 5—the piece to be used in the design starting from the edge, following the original weave and at the same time withdrawing the original cord. Follow the same procedure from the other side.

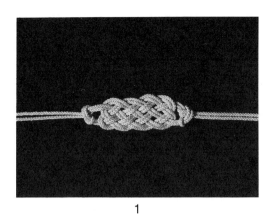

1

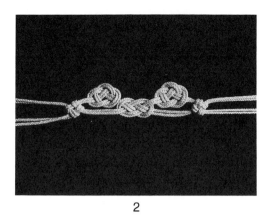

2

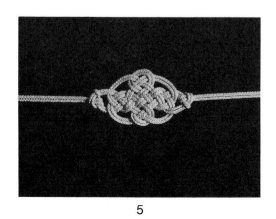

3

4

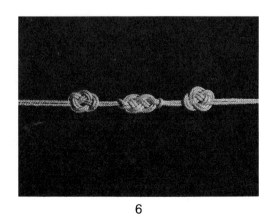

5

6

Women's Knotted Accessories

Key Ring: Figure 1. This is a handy nautical piece of knotwork that can be used by both men and women. It was made with 2 feet of 1/16-inch-diameter cord. The Turk's Head (page 56) is formed first with three passes. Then, rather than putting it over a pole, it is worked into a ball shape by slowly pulling out the slack. As it grows smaller, insert a small ball of cloth in its center to give it a little body. Continue to remove the slack until it is small and firm. Then finish it off with a whipping (page 62).

Hat Decoration: Figure 2. The Doubled Carrick Bend on a Bight (page 32) and alternate Figure-of-Eight Knots (page 48) were used in this ornament.

Barrettes: Figure 3. Made from the Doubled Carrick Bend Chain (page 74). The material required is 14 feet of 1/16-inch-diameter cord. This knot is held in place with a six-inch-long wood dowel.

Barrettes: Figure 4. Made by repeating the weave shown on page 86 several times. The material required is 20 feet of 1/16-inch-diameter cord. This knot was cemented to a metal clip similar to that shown on page 146, Figure 3.

Necklace: Figure 5. This design was made with Carrick Bends (page 36) alternating with Overhand Knots (page 40). It is finished off with a whipping (page 62), or the ends can be finished off with a jewelry clasp. It requires four pieces of 1/16-inch-diameter cord, each 8 feet long. The four pieces are pulled through the ornament until there are equal amounts on each side. Form the first Carrick Bend. Next, form an Overhand Knot with the left group and one with the right group. Proceed as shown in the illustration.

1

2

3

4

5

Knotted Belt Designs

Attractive belts can be quickly made by simply forming some of the knotted designs such as those illustrated on page 135. The belts can be made either small, as shown in Figure 1, or large, as illustrated in Figure 4. The designs can be varied by using colored cord or by using cord or rope of different sizes and materials.

Figure 1. This belt is made from the Lark's Head Carrick Bend. The method of forming it is shown on page 66. The material required is two pieces of rope, each 6 feet long and ¼ inch in diameter. This length will provide sufficient material to fit any waist.

Figure 2. The End Interlocking Carrick Bend was used to form this belt. See page 86 for details of forming the knot. The material required is two pieces of rope, each 9 feet long and ¼ inch in diameter.

Figure 3. The Interlocking Carrick Bend Wreath as illustrated on page 104 is used to form this design. It requires two pieces of rope, each 10 feet long and ⅛ inch in diameter. A larger figure can be made by using ¼-inch-diameter material.

Figure 4. You will frequently want to fashion a very large woven belt. This can be readily made by simply grouping several individual designs as may be found elsewhere in this book in the manner shown in this figure. The design is started from the left side by forming a Two-Strand Carrick Bend Weave (page 38). This is followed by the Half-Hitched Carrick Bend (page 64). The weave in the center is the Short Carrick Bend Mat (page 112). As you proceed to the right, you once again repeat the Half-Hitched Carrick Bend, followed by the Two-Strand Carrick Bend Weave. The ends are now used to tie the design around the waist. The material required is four pieces of rope, each 13 feet long and ¼ inch in diameter.

Additional belt weaves are illustrated on several of the following pages.

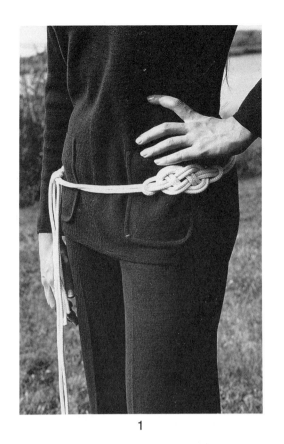

1

2

3

4

Additional Knotted Belt Designs

Figure 1. Start on the left with a Two-Strand Half-Hitched Carrick Bend (see page 64), followed by a Two-Strand Carrick Bend Weave (page 38), and another Two-Strand Half-Hitched Carrick Bend, the loops of which are joined as shown. The figure measures 9 inches wide and 7 inches high. Material required: four pieces of 1/4-inch-diameter rope, each 10 feet long. This allows sufficient material to be tied around the waist.

First 2. This weave was made entirely from the Half-Hitched Carrick Bend (page 64) and the Four-Strand Sennit Weave (page 49). It measures 7 inches wide and 7 inches high. Material required: two pieces of 1/4-inch-diameter rope, each 12 feet long.

Figure 3. Made in the same manner as Figure 1, except a Square Knot (page 44) is formed with the side loops of the Half-Hitched Carrick Bends. It measures 7 inches wide and 7 inches high. Material required: four pieces of 1/4-inch-diameter rope, each 10 feet long.

Figure 4. The basic knot used here is a Half-Hitched Carrick Bend (page 64). The side loops are woven in the form of a Caterpillar Knot (page 50). The design measures 8 inches wide and 5 inches high. Material required: four pieces of 1/4-inch-diameter rope, each 10 feet long.

Figure 5. Made by forming a Single Carrick Bend Chain (page 74). This is shown at the bottom of Figure 5 on page 137. When the desired belt length has been reached, then thread the two ends through the Carrick Bends as shown. Please note that the loops on the left-hand side of the belt have been purposely left short in order to properly illustrate the procedure in the photograph. The finished belt appears at the top of Figure 5. The ends are passed around the waist and tied through the loops. The belt is 2 inches wide and requires two pieces, each 20 feet long for a 30-inch waist. The material is 1/4-inch-diameter rope.

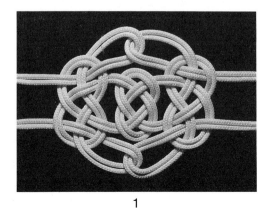

1

2

3

4

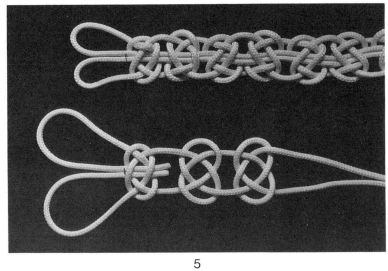

5

Additional Knotted Belt Designs

Figure 1. This weave is a variation of the Royal Carrick Bend (page 108). Follow the steps from Figures 1 through 6, at which point the weave is locked by over-and-under passes and will then appear as shown here. It measures 7 inches wide and 4 inches high, and requires two pieces of ¼-inch-diameter rope, each 10 feet long.

Figure 2. First form the Two-Strand Carrick Bend Weave in the center (page 38). With the two groups of two ropes on the left, weave a Royal Carrick Bend (page 111, Figure 21). Repeat this on the right-hand side to complete the design, which measures 14 inches wide and 7 inches high. This belt requires four pieces of ¼-inch-diameter rope, each 13 feet long.

Figure 3. Form a Two-Strand Half-Hitched Carrick Bend (page 64) and leave several inches of slack in the loops. Follow with a Two-Strand Carrick Bend Weave (page 38), passing the ends through the upper loops, and then form another Two-Strand Half-Hitched Carrick Bend. The weave measures 10 inches wide and 7 inches high, and requires four pieces of ¼-inch-diameter rope, each 11 feet long.

Figure 4. The girdle weave is started from the top center with the Four-Strand Sennit Weave (page 49). This is followed with a series of Doubled Carrick Bend Chains (page 74), up to the desired belt length. It can then be tied in front with either a Two-Strand Carrick Bend Weave, as shown, or a Square Knot (page 46). This belt is 3 inches wide and requires four pieces of ¼-inch-diameter rope, each 14 feet long, to fit a 30-inch waist.

Figure 5. This design is started from the center with Two-Strand Carrick Bend Weave (page 38). This is followed by a Doubled Carrick Bend Chain (page 74) on each side. It measures 15 inches wide and 3 inches high, and requires four pieces of ¼-inch-diameter rope, each 11 feet long.

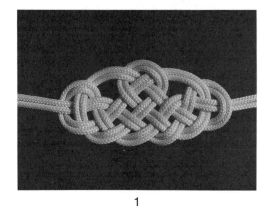

1

2

3

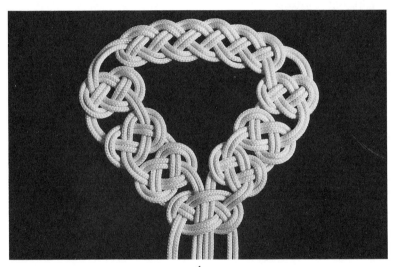

4

5

The Side Interlocking Carrick Bend Belt

This belt (page 141, Figure 1) was made with ⅛-inch-diameter cord. The method of weaving it is illustrated in detail on page 72 (Side Interlocking Carrick Bend).

It requires 7 inches of cord to make each inch of knotted belt. Therefore, if the waist is 30 inches, multiply 30 by 7 to equal 210 inches. This will yield 30 inches of knotted belt. To this, add about 24 inches of cord to provide the extra length needed to tie the belt around the waist.

Note: When the belt is made with doubled cord as illustrated, two cords this length are required.

Each end of the knotted portion of the belt is finished off by tying an Over-hand Knot as shown on page 40 at the first Carrick Bend loop, and also in the last one as shown. The extreme ends of the cords are finished off with a Figure-of-Eight Knot decoration (see page 48).

This belt can be made in a more open weave by using a single strand as shown on page 72. A heavier belt can be made by using three strands.

Another variation is to use two or even three different colors of cord in the belt, finishing off the ends with a tassel as shown on page 58.

The design illustrated on page 141, Figure 2, can be used as a neck choker or as a bracelet.

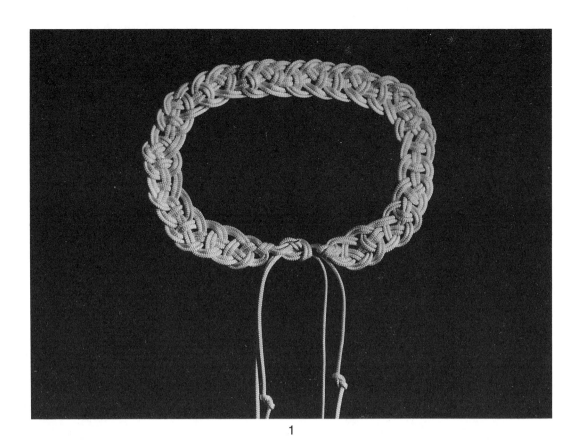

1

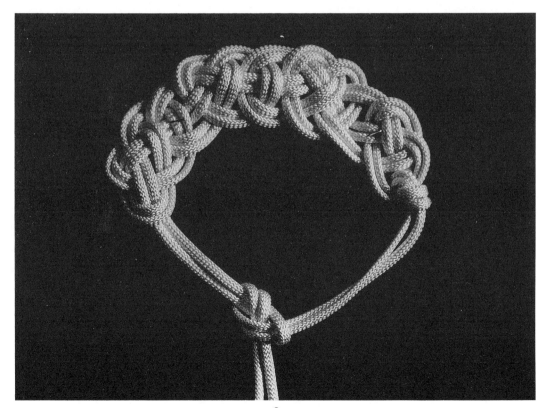

2

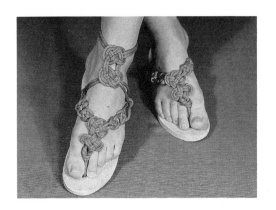
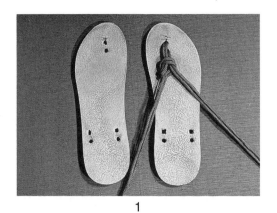

1

Sandal Binding

Ornamental knots applied to a rubber or leather sole form a functional set of footwear, as illustrated above. The ends of the cords can be cut off short, after the knots have been tied, or they can be left long and tied around the leg, for a Roman effect.

Two pieces of ⅛-inch-diameter cord are required, each 4 feet long, or, if the Roman type is desired, 6 feet long. This provides enough material for a small size. For a medium size, add 2 feet, and for large, add 4 feet. Six holes are made in the sole as shown in Figure 1.

The weave is started by doubling over the two pieces of cord, pulling them through the front two holes and tying an Overhand Knot (page 40) with two strands, as in Figure 1. Next tie a doubled Dragonfly Knot (page 52), followed by a Two-Strand Carrick Bend Weave (page 38). With each pair of strands form two Carrick Bends (page 28). (At this point, if a larger sandal binding is desired, simply add additional Carrick Bends.) The work at this point appears as in Figure 2. The final step is to pull the cord ends through the rear holes and finish them off as in Figure 3, with a long whipping (page 62).

2

3

Pocketbook

The materials used to fashion articles with the Carrick Bend are almost limitless. For example, the handbag illustrated above is made with shoelaces.

The design measures 8 inches wide and 8 inches high and requires thirty-two flat shoelaces (as long as possible). Thirty of these are used for the bag and two for the drawstrings.

The work is started from the bottom of the bag by tying a Square Knot (page 44) with two shoelaces as shown on the left of Figure 1. This is repeated until all thirty laces are used—there will now be fifteen sets. Take two sets and tie Carrick Bends in them (page 28), as shown on the right of Figure 1. Continue adding one set at a time to the edge until all fifteen sets have been used. Next, lay the work over a book about the size of this one, with all Square Knots on the top edge, and the laces hanging down. Continue tying Carrick Bends in the manner shown in Figure 2.

Note: When working with a flat material it should be folded in order to *lie* properly (carefully study Figure 2). When all the material has been used in the knot-tying operation, the ends are tied to the drawstrings with an Overhand Knot (page 40). The bag can then be used as is or a lining sewn in as illustrated.

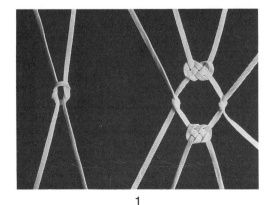

1

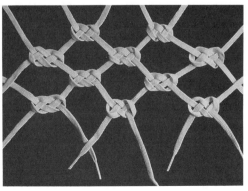

2

The Carrick Bend Frogs

A handmade frog applied to women's clothing will give that "rich" look such as no other form of ornamentation can achieve. Yet it is very easy and inexpensive to make.

The best material to use is rayon piping which is stitched down the center the long way on a sewing machine. This slightly flattens the piping, makes it a little wider, and gives it a more pleasing appearance when the knot is finished.

It should be noted that two pieces are required, one with a button (Figure 6) and one with a loop (Figure 8). The frog is started by forming the Carrick Bend on a Bight (page 30). This is made quite small and pushed into a cap fashion as shown in Figure 2. As this is done, the knot is pulled up tighter until all the slack has been removed and the knot appears as a ball and is quite firm (Figure 3). This forms the button. Next, sew the edges of the two strands together for about 1⅓ inches, starting from just below the button, and then forming another Carrick Bend. The knot will now appear as in Figure 4. Form the bottom loop as shown in Figure 5. The ends are sewn together (see page 71) and cut off short. This finishes one half.

The other half of the frog is made by taking the center of another piece of piping and forming a loop as shown in Figure 7. Again sew the two edges of the cords together, leaving a loop just large enough for the button to pass through. Then continue by weaving a Carrick Bend as before and finishing off the ends in the same manner (Figure 8).

The two halves are now joined as pictured above, placed in the desired location on the garment, and sewn into place. The frog set above was made with ¼-inch-diameter material and required two pieces, each 3 feet long. It measures 8 inches wide and 3 inches high.

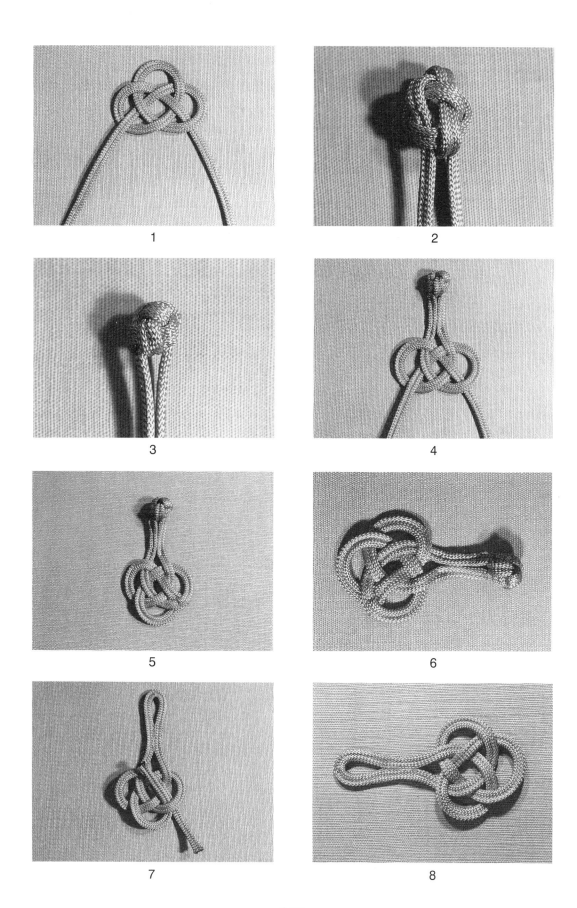

1

2

3

4

5

6

7

8

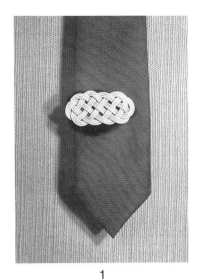

1

2

Tie Clips and Tacks

The knot used for the tie clip shown in Figure 1 is the Short Carrick Bend Mat (page 112). The knot used for the tie tack shown in Figure 2 is the Carrick Bend Coaster (page 68). Both knots were made out of 80-pound test (this is the size) fishing line. This should not be made out of the monofilament type of line (although it can be). I prefer the kind that is twisted of three strands into a single cord. This gives the design more of that "ropey" nautical look. The design in Figure 1 measures 2 inches wide, and the design in Figure 2 measures three-quarters of an inch in width.

The blank metal parts used to mount the knots can be purchased at a hobby or handicraft supply store, and are illustrated in Figures 3 and 4. The knot is prepared by placing it *face* down and "buttering" the back with a *clear* epoxy adhesive. Then butter the face of the metal clip with adhesive and place the clip on the knot. Turn the whole assembly over so the clip is on the bottom and the knot is on top. Place in a support and let dry.

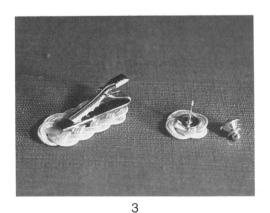

3

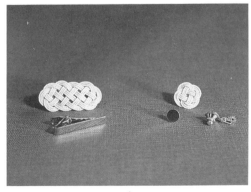

4

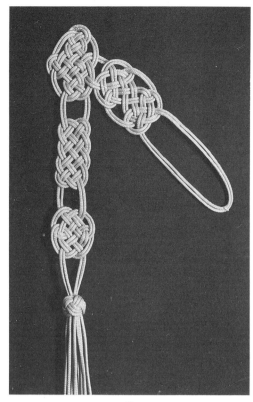

1

2

Curtain Tiebacks

An unusual set of drapery and curtain tiebacks can be fashioned with ornamental knots in the manner shown above in Figure 1.

The design measures 7 inches wide at the top and 24 inches long. It requires ⅛-inch-diameter cord: two pieces, each 20 feet long; six pieces, each 2 feet long for tassels; and one piece 6 feet long for the Turk's Head.

Start with a Four-Strand Sennit Carrick Bend (page 92), as shown at upper right-hand side of Figure 2. (Note that a loop about 6 inches long must be left.) Follow with a Royal Carrick Bend (pages 108 and 111), with the ends coming from the side of the knot rather than the bottom. The Short Carrick Bend Mat is now formed (page 112), followed by the End Interlocking Carrick Bend (page 86). Finish off the design by doubling over the six 2-foot-long pieces and forming a tassel (see pages 59 and 60, Figures 6, 7, 8, and 9). The final step is to cover the top of the tassel with a Carrick Bend Turk's Head (page 56), using the 6-foot piece.

Vary the tieback by using any combination of knots and choosing colored cords to complement the drapes.

147

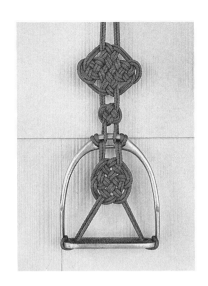

The Stirrup Hanging

This design can be used as a wall hanging, or a wood shelf can be placed between the stirrups to make a most unusual window display for plantings. Each stirrup requires two ropes, ⅛ inch in diameter, and each 10 feet long.

Take the center of each rope and loop it around the bottom of each side of the stirrup as shown top right. Next, form the End Interlocking Carrick Bend (page 86) in the center of the stirrup,
followed by lacing the ends through the upper part as pictured. Next, make a Two-Strand Carrick Bend Weave (page 38), and then form a Royal Carrick Bend (page 108). The hanging is finished off, determining the desired length of the upper ropes as shown upper left. Then apply a seizing as shown in Figure 1 to fasten the ends (page 61). Conceal the seizing by covering it with a Carrick Bend Turk's Head (page 56).

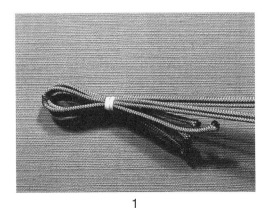

1

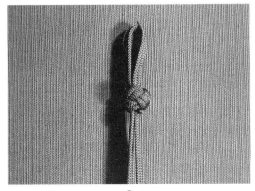

2

Carrick Bend Doormat

Doormats require a greater amount of heavier rope than is usually used in ornamental knotwork. The mat pictured here measures 11 inches wide and 20 inches long and was made with ½-inch-diameter braided nylon rope.

The material required is 80 feet of ½-inch-diameter rope, which can be either nylon, Dacron, manila, or hemp.

Instructions for making the weave will be found on page 112. The mat illustrated was made with 5 passes, which provide the bulk for the large size.

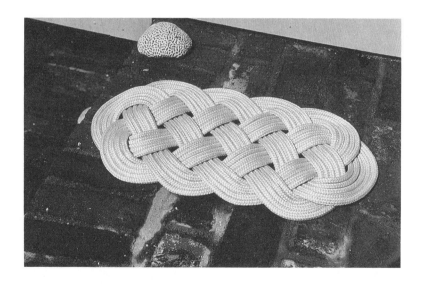

The Knotted Picture Frame

The design illustrated on page 151 measures 16 inches wide by 19 inches high. It forms an excellent framing for either awards or nautical pictures. The entire frame was covered with knots, made of 1/8-inch-diameter braided nylon rope. Knots other than those shown here can, of course, be used in designing your own knotted frame covering. And a wider knot design can be used over the entire area, such as that at the bottom of Figure 1.

The first step is to either make or purchase a plain wood frame of a suitable size. The type used to mount artists' canvas is perfect. The wood is then covered with fabric, such as an old sheet. Wrap it around like a bandage, as in Figure 2.

The knotwork for the top and each side are now made separately. The knots used are a continuous chain of alternating Two-Strand Carrick Bend Weaves (page 38) and Dragonfly Knots (page 52). The knots are made using four strands of rope; 5 inches of material are required for each 1 inch of knotted frame covering. When the necessary lengths have been made, first apply the top piece and sew it to the fabric covering the wood, and then cut off any surplus in the corners. Repeat this procedure on each of the sides.

The bottom weave is made last, starting from the center, with two Four-Strand Sennit Weaves (page 49), followed by the End Interlocking Carrick Bend (page 86). However, instead of finishing off the weave by locking it as shown in Figure 7, it should be left in the unlocked position as in Figure 1 and the weaving continued until the required length has been made. At this point the weave is locked as in Figure 8. This piece is now applied to the frame, sewn in place, and the surplus on the ends cut off. The corner will now appear as shown in Figure 3. This part of the knotwork requires four pieces of 1/8-inch-diameter rope, each 14 feet long, for each side.

The final step is to cover the raw ends in the corners. This is done with a small "patch" type of knot. On the top corners of the frame, a Carrick Bend Coaster (page 68); on the bottom corners, a Royal Carrick Bend (page 108). These are now applied to the frame and sewn into place.

You will now have completed (at a very nominal cost) a project which will be a delight to have in any home.

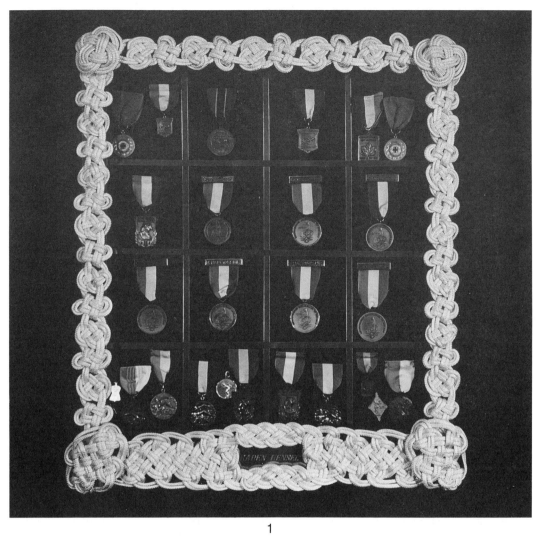

1

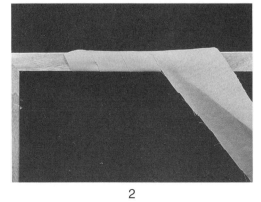

2

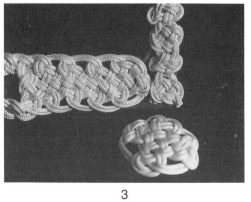

3

Carrick Bend Hot Pad

This design was fashioned from the Doubled Carrick Bend Chain (page 74). There are eight knots formed, which are then shaped into a circle; the ends are joined, sewn in back, and cut off as shown on page 71 (Figures 19 and 20).

The figure illustrated below measures 10 inches in diameter. The material required is two pieces of $1/4$-inch-diameter rope, each 9 feet long.

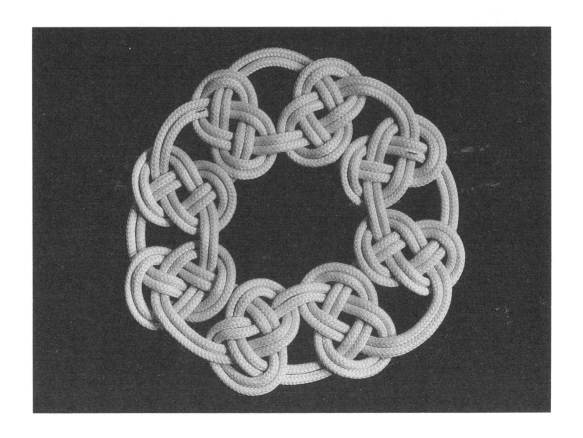

Carrick Bend Table Mat

This attractive and functional knot can be made in about twenty minutes. This is one of the nice things about doing Carrick Bend ornamental knotting: it is possible to create interesting designs in a very short time.

The mat design can also be used as a hot pad for tabletop protection or as an ornamental wall hanging.

The figure illustrated below measures 9 inches in diameter. The material required is one piece of rope 17 feet in length and $7/16$ of an inch in diameter. Note that this design was fashioned with two-color braided rope to create a very unusual effect in the knotted work.

It was made from the End Interlocking Carrick Bend (page 86), except that instead of weaving with two pieces it was started with an Unlocked Carrick Bend on a Bight (page 34). When the basic knot has been tied, it is then doubled as described on page 68.

154

The Ship's Anchor

The anchor pictured on page 154 is an excellent example of the design possibilities that can be executed when variations on the Carrick Bend are used. The anchor measures 12 inches wide and 18 inches high.

The rope required is two pieces each 18 feet long, two pieces each 30 feet long, and one piece 8 feet long, all ⅛ inch in diameter.

The design is started by first making the ring at the top of the anchor, beginning from the middle of one 30-foot-long piece. It is formed from an Interlocking Carrick Bend Wreath (page 104). At the bottom of the ring, form a doubled Fig-

ure-of-Eight with the two ends (page 48). (See Figure 2, page 155.) Below this, form a single Hanging Epaulet Weave (page 82). The other 30-foot piece is now threaded through the design just below the Figure-of-Eight, as shown in Figure 1, and traced through, to double the Hanging Epaulet Weave, so it appears as in Figure 2. This now provides two sets of two ropes, which are used to form the four doubled Japanese Crown Knots (page 54), with a Caterpillar Knot (page 50) separating each one in the order shown in Figures 3 and 4 below. This completes the stem or shank of the anchor.

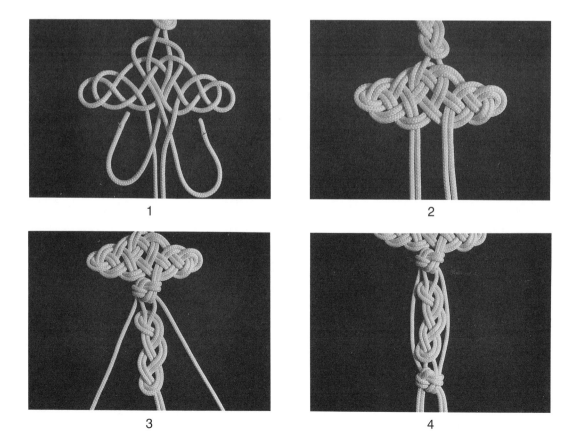

1

2

3

4

The next step is to weave the bottom, or flukes, which is done by first weaving a Long Carrick Bend Mat "trace" design (see pages 112 and 115, and note below) with separate pieces of rope. Place it at the bottom of the stem in the manner shown in Figure 5. The tracing procedure is now started as shown in Figures 6 through 8. Then you remove one of the trace ropes and the design will appear as in Figure 9. At this point only one-half of the Long Carrick Bend Mat has been traced and another pair is required to complete the knot. This pair, the two pieces 18 feet long, is used to trace through the remainder of the mat, starting at the bottom center as in Figure 11 and continuing as in Figure 12. The remaining trace rope should now be removed. The knot shall be pulled up and blocked (as described on page 20). It will now appear as in Figure 13. The flukes are finished by weaving a Short

Carrick Bend Mat on each side (Figure 14) and a Hanging Epaulet Weave (pages 112 and 82). The ends are then sewn and cut off as shown on page 71.

The final step is to double over the 8-foot piece and attach it to the ring (page 154). The two pieces are now twisted (to simulate a large rope), and finished off with a Carrick Bend Coaster (page 68).

The anchor, put on a suitable mounting surface, is manipulated into the proper shape and stapled in place (page 26). The finished design appears on page 154.

Note: It is very difficult to weave some designs when starting at points other than those shown in this book. It is, therefore, necessary to first form the weave with separate ropes to make the pattern used to trace the knot. The trace design ropes are removed once the knot has been duplicated.

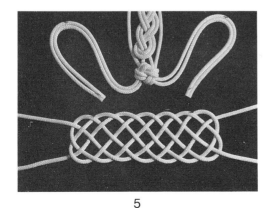

5

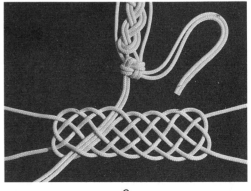

6

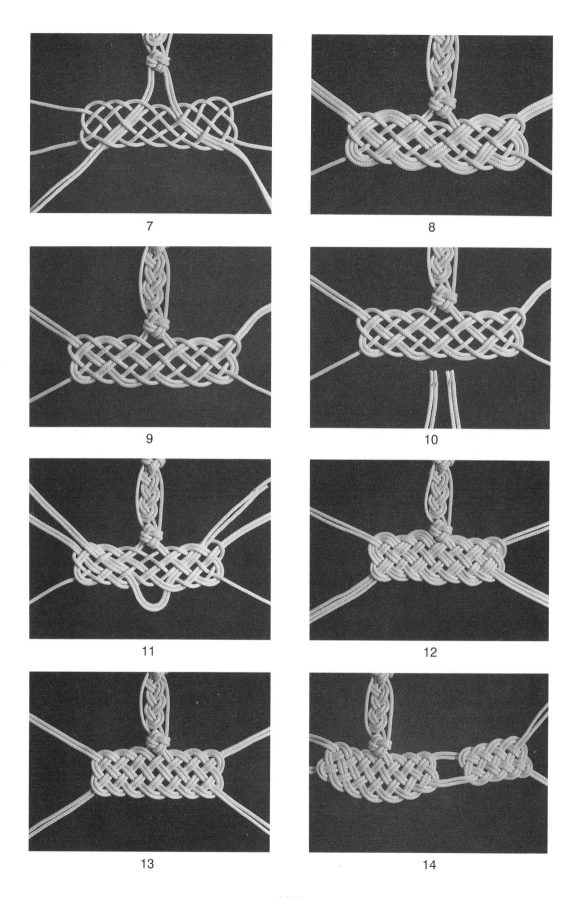

7

8

9

10

11

12

13

14

The Hanging Bottle Weave

An ordinary bottle can be transformed into a work of art quite easily. Although it may look difficult it is a simple process to make the design shown above.

The material required is four pieces of cord, ⅛-inch in diameter, each 14 feet long. These are doubled over as shown in Figures 1 and 2. Join two pieces as shown in Figure 3 (a Square Knot) and proceed to insert the other cords through it as shown in Figures 4 through 10.

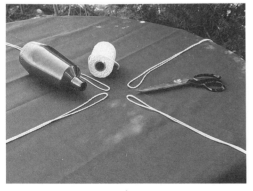

1

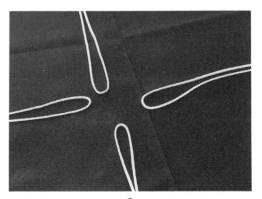

2

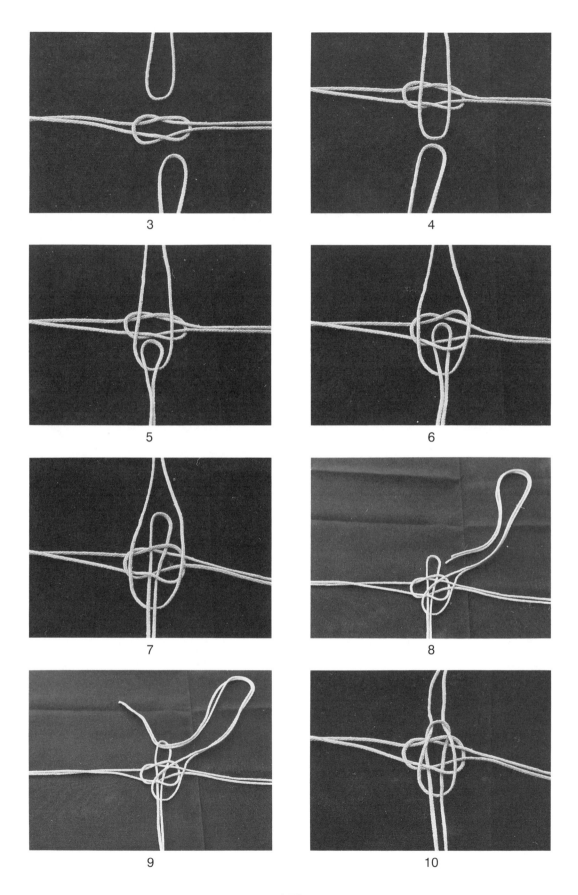

3

4

5

6

7

8

9

10

The two interlocking Square Knots are now pulled up taut (Figure 11). Next, tie four Carrick Bends (page 28) as shown in Figure 12. The work is now transferred to the bottle bottom (Figure 13) and secured in place with adhesive tape (Figures 14 and 15). Position the bottle *bottom up* and continue weaving Carrick Bends, starting as shown in Figure 16.

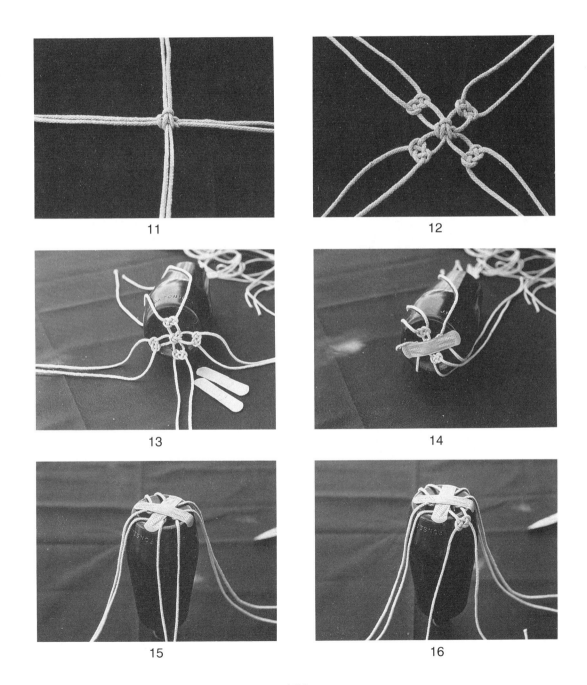

11

12

13

14

15

16

The Carrick Bend knots are continued down the face of the bottle as shown in Figures 17 through 21. Note that each row of knots is formed by tying it with one cord from each of the previously formed Carrick Bends. Space them symmetrically around the bottle before pulling them up snug. (Notice they are pulled up snug, *not tight*. A tight knot loses its shape.)

The final step is to tie additional Carrick Bends around the neck of the bottle (Figure 22), simply by tying the knots closer together. A bottle of any shape can be covered by spacing the knots closer together or farther apart.

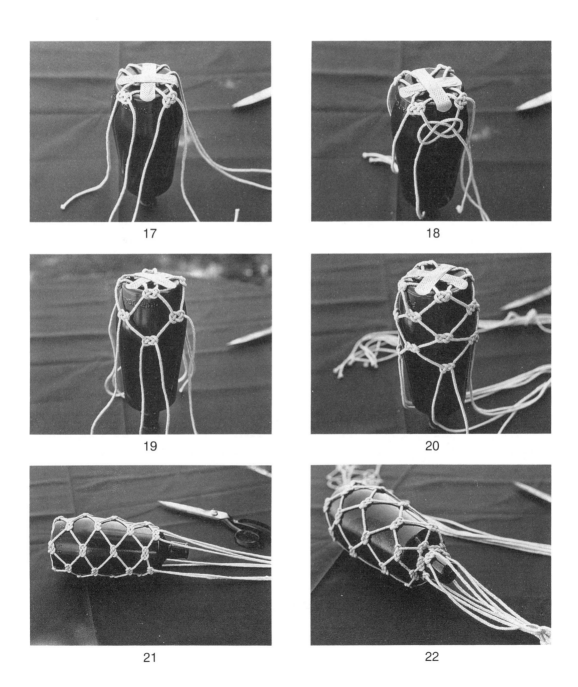

17

18

19

20

21

22

Additional Hanging Bottle Weaves

If you don't know what to do with used bottles, then fashion them into hanging ornaments for display in a window, as illustrated above. Any size, shape, or color will do. The entire bottle can be used, or it can be cut in half like the one above right. If all clear-glass bottles are used, any color combination can be made simply by filling the bottle with colored water. In addition, colored cord can be used, such as Figure 2, which is all red, and Figure 3, which is half red and half white.

The method of covering the bottles in each case is the same as that illustrated on pages 158 through 161, except that some of the knot combinations have been changed, as described below.

Figure 1. This bottle requires four pieces of 1/8-inch-diameter rope, each 14 feet long, which are doubled over as shown on page 158, Figure 2, to start the work. The knot used here is the Two-Strand Carrick Bend Weave (page 38).

Figure 2. This one requires four pieces of 1/8-inch-diameter rope, each 20 feet long. All knots are the same as those used on page 158, except for the center design, which is the Interlocking Carrick Bend Wreath (page 104).

When the bottle has been covered, cut off 2 feet of the end of the ropes, thread half of these through the weave on each side of the bottle, and form a tassel as shown on page 58.

Figure 3. This bottle weave requires two red and two white ropes, each 18 feet long. The knots used are the same as those on page 158, with the addition of some Overhand Knots (page 40). When the bottle has been covered, cut off 2 feet of the ends of the ropes and form a tassel on the bottom (page 58).

Figure 4. This bottle was cut in half, leaving the top open for a flower arrangement. The material required is four pieces of 1/8-inch rope, each 14 feet long. The knots used in the weave are the Carrick Bend (page 28), the Figure-of-Eight (page 48), and the Dragonfly Knot (page 52).

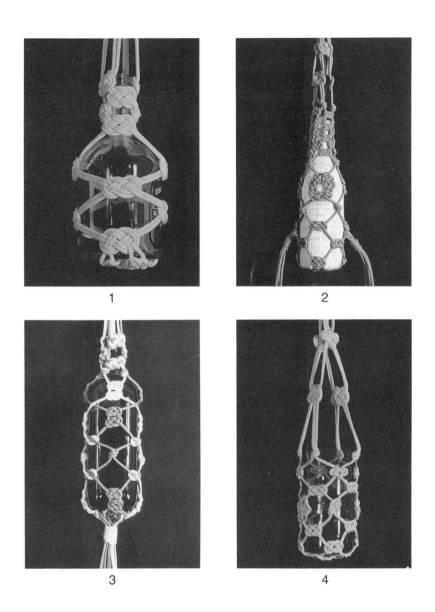

1

2

3

4

The Hanging Basket Weave

This weave was made around a copper pot which was 12 inches in diameter. Six pieces of rope are required, each 20 feet long by ⅛ inch in diameter, and one curtain ring about 1½ inches in diameter. Each rope is doubled over and attached to the ring with a Lark's Head Knots (Figures 1-3). Three Two-Strand Carrick Bend Weaves are formed as shown in Figure 5 (page 38). Next, divide the strands and form six single Carrick Bends (Figure 6), which are then fastened to the bottom of the pot with adhesive tape (Figure 7). The tape holds the weave until the operation is completed. It is then removed. Continue weaving single Carrick Bends as shown in Figure 8, spacing each knot uniformly. Added ornamentation can be introduced, such as the Hanging Epaulet Weave in Figure 9 (page 82). Additional Carrick Bends are now added to finish the design (Figure 10). The assembly is turned over and some Overhand Knots (page 40) are tied with all the strands as shown above.

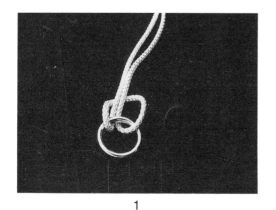

1

2

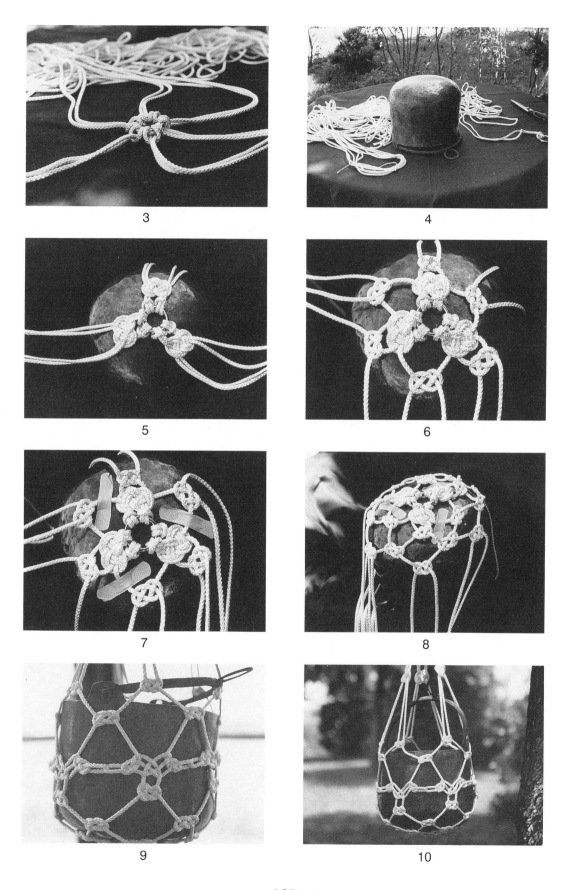

3

4

5

6

7

8

9

10

165

Decorative Ropework

Ornament Frame: Figure 1. A suggested method of framing a nautical object to give it a salty flavor. The material required is three pieces of cord ⅛ inch in diameter, each 14 feet long. The design measures 9 inches wide and 12 inches high. It is formed with Side Interlocking Carrick Bends (page 72).

Lamp Shade Decorations: Figure 2. The Carrick Bend on a Bight knots (page 30) were made with three strands of heavy all-purpose rug yarn, which is similar to knitting yarn, only heavier. Each knot requires a 2-foot length of the triple yarn and each one measures 3½ inches wide and 2½ inches high with a 2-inch space between. The large Carrick Bend on a Bight was made with five pieces of yarn, each 4 feet long; the design measures 6 inches wide and 6 inches high.

Room Divider: Figure 3. This measures 2 feet wide and 7 feet long. The material required is 576 feet of ¼-inch-diameter rope. The rope is cut in 12 lengths, each 48 feet long. Each piece is doubled over and hung on a wooden pole. There are now 12 sets of two strands, each strand 24 feet long. From this point on, any combination of knots can be used and in any order. The following knot weaves were used in fashioning this divider, starting from the top:

Two-Strand Carrick Bend
   Weave   Page 38
Figure-of-Eight   Page 48
Hanging Epaulet Weave   Page 82
Variation of the Interlocking
   Carrick Bend Wreath   Page 104
Carrick Bend with two
   strands passed through
   the center   Page 28
End Interlocking Carrick
   Bend   Page 86
Back of the Japanese
   Crown Knot   Page 54
Dragonfly Knot   Page 52

1

2

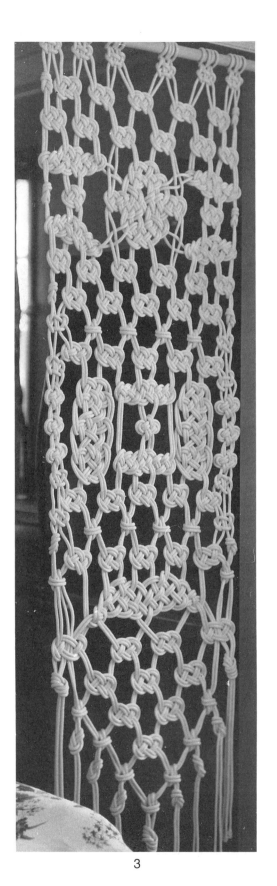

3

Carrick Bend Variations

The designs that can be formed with the Carrick Bend are almost endless. Some of the variations and combinations are illustrated on the following pages. Once the basic Carrick Bend knot has been learned, the examples illustrated here will be quite simple to execute.

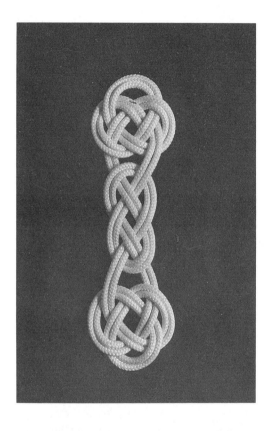

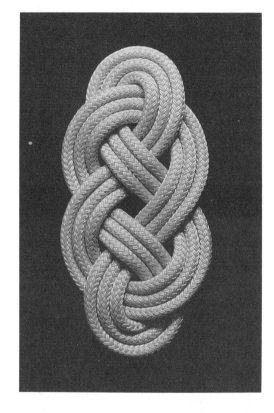

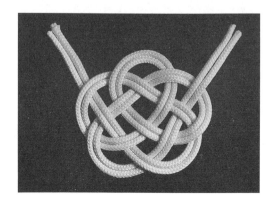

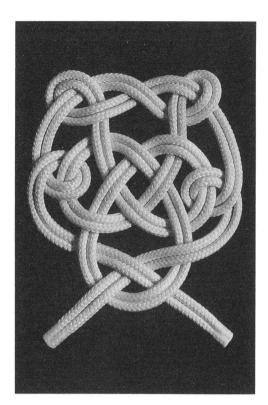

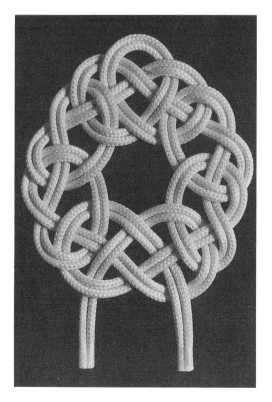

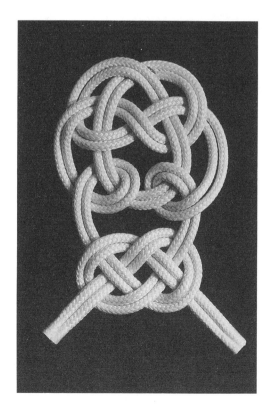

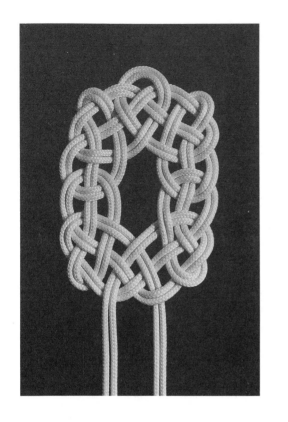

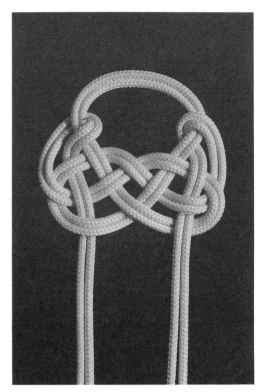

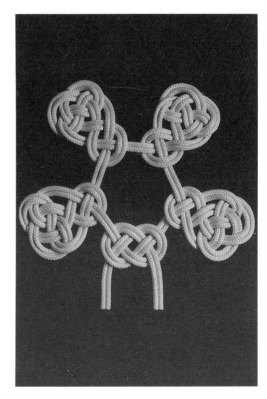

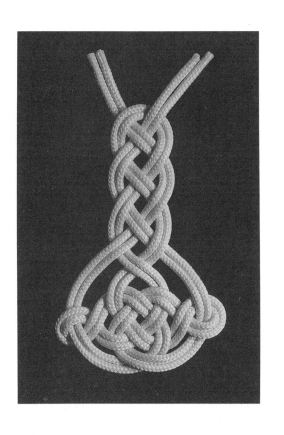

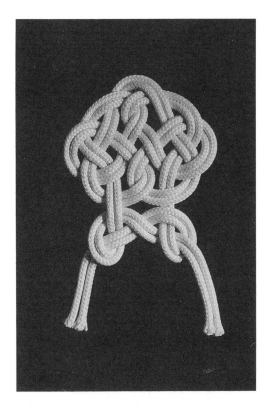

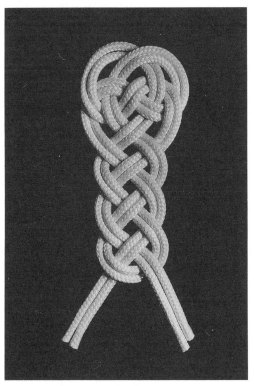

1. 3-strand mason, fish line, polished cotton, or seine twine.
2. Chainette
3. Venetian blind cord.
4. Rattail.
5. ⅛-inch-diameter braided halyard line.
6. ⅛-inch-diameter tubular braid.
7. ⅛-inch-diameter piping.
8. ³⁄₁₆-inch-diameter red and white Dacron, braided rope.
9. ¼-inch-diameter green and white Dacron, braided rope.
10. ¼-inch-diameter Dacron, braided rope.
11. ¼-inch-diameter piping.
12. ⁵⁄₁₆-inch-diameter manila 3-strand rope.
13. ⅜-inch-diameter blue nylon 3-strand rope.
14. ¼-inch-diameter heavy wool or acrylic yarn.
15. ⅜-inch-diameter blue nylon braided rope.
16. ½-inch-diameter blue nylon 3-strand rope.

Other materials can be used as required to suit the design being fashioned.

Note: The pencil is for size comparison.

Material Supply Sources

Materials for fashioning articles illustrated in *The Book of Ornamental Knots* are available from many sources. The yellow pages of your local telephone directory can supply names and addresses of many of the following:

    Marine equipment and supplies
    Marinas
    Hardware stores
    Rope suppliers
    Twine and cordage suppliers
    Craft shops

    Passementerie shops
(novelty cordage)
    Dress trimmings
    Department stores

In addition to the above, craft magazines and marine supply catalogues are excellent sources of material vendors.

Many examples in this book are best made of old rope, which presents a pleasing antique look. This material can often be found in marinas where boat owners frequently discard their worn-out lines.

Index